A PERFORMER'S GUIDE TO MUSIC *of* THE Baroque Period

Series Editor
Anthony Burton

ABRSM

First published in 2002 by
The Associated Board of the Royal Schools of Music (Publishing) Limited,
a wholly owned subsidiary of ABRSM,
24 Portland Place, London W1B 1LU, United Kingdom

Reprinted in 2003, 2007, 2009, 2010

© 2002 by The Associated Board of the Royal Schools of Music

ISBN 978 1 86096 192 2

AB 2764

A CIP catalogue for this book is available from The British Library.

Design and formatting by Geoffrey Wadsley
Music origination by Jack Thompson
CD compilation and mastering by Ken Blair (BMP Recording)
Printed in England by Halstan & Co. Ltd, Amersham, Bucks

#59499400

Contents

Illustrations

Notes on the Contributors

Christopher Hogwood, CBE, is the director of The Academy of Ancient Music, which he founded in 1973, and which has consistently been in the forefront of historically informed music-making. He conducts concerts and opera all over the world, both with specialist period ensembles and with orchestras of modern instruments. His vast catalogue of recordings includes performances not only as conductor and director but also as a soloist on harpsichord and clavichord. He has published many editions and articles, and books including a guide to the trio sonata and a biography of Handel.

George Pratt is emeritus professor and formerly head of the department of music in the University of Huddersfield; he now divides his time between lecturing, continuo playing, reviewing CDs and broadcasting. He has conducted and directed student orchestras and Baroque ensembles. As well as many articles and editions, he has published books on school music teaching and on the development of aural skills.

Peter Holman founded the pioneering early music group Ars Nova while studying with Thurston Dart at King's College, London. He is now director of The Parley of Instruments, with which he has made numerous record-ings, director of the choir Psalmody, and musical director of Opera Restor'd. Much in demand as a teacher and lecturer in Britain, Europe and the USA, he is reader in historical musicology at Leeds University, and consultant in period performance at the Royal Northern College of Music, Manchester. His writings include *Four and Twenty Fiddlers: The Violin at the English Court 1540–1690*, and a study of the music of Purcell.

Davitt Moroney is one of the world's leading players of historical keyboard instruments, with nearly fifty CDs to his credit; he is a specialist in the music of Bach, in the French harpsichord school, and in English keyboard music from Byrd to Purcell. British-born, he now divides his time between Paris and Berkeley, California, where he holds a professorial post and is also University organist. For ABRSM (Publishing) Ltd he has edited the 'Purcell manuscript' discovered in 1993, and written a short biography of Bach.

Andrew Manze is widely known for his performances and recordings of Baroque music, as a solo violinist, chamber musician and director. Formerly associate director of The Academy of Ancient Music, he was appointed director of The English Concert in 2002; he also makes frequent guest appearances with both period-instrument ensembles and orchestras of modern instruments. He is a tutor and director of the European Union

Baroque Orchestra, and a visiting professor at the Royal College of Music, London.

Stephen Preston has played a leading role in the early music movement in Britain and abroad, as a solo flautist and a leading member of The English Concert, The Academy of Ancient Music and other ensembles. He has also extended his interest in historically informed performance to the field of dance, most recently with his company MZT. He works regularly with student instrumentalists and singers in London and the USA.

John Potter was a member of the Hilliard Ensemble for seventeen years, and is a co-founder of Red Byrd; with these groups and as a solo tenor he has made more than a hundred CDs, many of them of music of the Baroque period. A lecturer in music at the University of York, he is the author of *Vocal Authority*, and editor of *The Cambridge Companion to Singing*.

Clifford Bartlett worked in the library of the Royal Academy of Music and the BBC music library before establishing King's Music to publish facsimiles and editions of early music. His editions are widely used by orchestras, choirs, ensembles and opera companies in Britain and abroad. He is also a regular reviewer of new publications of early music, and a keyboard continuo player.

Anthony Burton studied music at Cambridge University, and worked as an arts administrator in New England and in Manchester before spending fifteen years as a music producer and manager for BBC Radio 3. He is now a freelance broadcaster and writer, covering a wide range of musical subjects. He was guest artistic director of the 2001 Spitalfields Festival in east London.

Acknowledgements

Acknowledgement for permission to reproduce illustrations and music examples is due to the following:

Illustrations
AKG, London: Figs 3.1, 3.4, 5.1
The British Library, London: Figs 4.3, 5.5
Fitzwilliam Museum, University of Cambridge/The Bridgeman Art Library, London: Fig. 5.2
Getty Images, London: Fig. 1.3
Kungliga Biblioteket. Bibliotheque Royale, Stockholm: Fig. 1.2
Lebrecht Music Collection, London: Figs 1.4, 5.3
Maidstone Museum & Bentlif Art Gallery: Fig. 3.3
Musée du Louvre, Paris/RMN/Gerard Blot: Fig. 5.4
Private Collection/The Bridgeman Art Library, London: Fig. 6.1
SCALA: Fig. 1.1
The State Hermitage Museum, St Petersburg: Fig. 4.2
Victoria & Albert Museum, London: Fig. 3.2

Music examples
The British Library, London: Exx. 2.18, 3.3
Cardiff Public Libraries, on permanent loan to Cardiff University: Ex. 2.21
Fitzwilliam Museum, University of Cambridge: Ex. 2.17a
Lebrecht Music Collection, London: Exx. 3.5, 6.4, 6.5, 6.6
© Copyright 1959 Novello & Co. Ltd, revised edition © 1990 Novello & Co. Ltd. All rights reserved. International copyright secured. Reproduced by permission: Ex. 2.2
© Copyright 1959 Novello & Co. Ltd, © renewed 1987, revised edition © 1992 Novello & Co. Ltd. All rights reserved. International copyright secured. Reproduced by permission: Ex. 6.3
© Oxford University Press 1968. Extract reproduced by permission: Ex. 2.1
© 1991 SCHOTT MUSIC Ltd, London. Reproduced by permission: Ex. 3.2
Staats- und Universitätsbibliothek, Hamburg (M B/1657). Reproduced by permission: Ex. 2.17b
Reproduced by permission of Stainer & Bell Ltd, London, England: Exx. 7.1, 7.3
Reproduced by permission of Thomson Publishing Services from Thurston Dart, *The Interpretation of Music* (London: Hutchinson's University Library, 1954): Ex. 2.16

Front and back covers
Woman at the Clavichord, c.1665, by Gerrit Dou (1613–75): Dulwich Picture Gallery, London/The Bridgeman Art Library, London.

General Notes

Where appropriate, note pitches are described using the Helmholtz system:

In the captions to the music examples, the date refers to composition unless given in brackets, in which case it is the date of publication or, in the case of stage works, first performance.

The symbol ⑩ is a cross-reference to the accompanying CD and the Notes on the CD on pp. 127–30.

Anthony Burton

Preface

What does it mean if you have played or sung a piece, and a friend, or a teacher, or an adjudicator, comments: 'That had a good sense of style'; or maybe 'That wasn't very stylish'? It means that the piece was performed with – or without – an understanding of how the composer would have expected it to sound at the time it was written. And it is to help you to find out what composers would have expected in different periods, and to apply your knowledge to your own playing or singing, that these Performer's Guides have been written.

In fact, until the early twentieth century the idea of 'period style' hardly existed. When music of the seventeenth or eighteenth centuries was revived it was usually treated, by editors and performers, as if it belonged to the present day. But as the century went on, musicians began to realize that they could not safely assume that everything – including instruments, and ways of playing them – had simply been getting better all the time, and so that their usual performing style was bound to suit any piece of music equally well.

They began to look for ways of performing music of the past with greater regard for the composer's expectations: through the revival of instruments like the harpsichord and the lute, and the formation of chamber orchestras; through a growth in 'Urtext' editions, which showed (or claimed to show) nothing but the composer's intentions; through the detailed study of 'performance practice', the way music was interpreted at different times and in different places; and more recently through the widespread use of instruments of the same period as the music (or, more often than not, exact modern copies). In all this, recordings played a major part, opening up many neglected areas of musical history, as well as throwing new light on well-known works by demonstrating how their composers might have expected them to sound.

For a while, these developments led to a dismaying move to leave whole areas of repertoire to the specialists: to frown on any performance of Baroque music on the piano; to remove not just Bach and Handel, but even Haydn and Mozart, from the programmes of symphony orchestras. But this was hardly fair to the performers or to their audiences; and for students wishing to get to know a wide range of music, probably without any chance of access to period instruments, it made no sense at all. In any case, as specialist performers and scholars extended their researches into the more familiar territory of the nineteenth century, they discovered that here too there were performing traditions which have been lost or misunderstood. So it has become increasingly clear that all performances of music of the past can benefit from the knowledge and experience gained by the 'early music movement'.

One area which has lagged behind in this has been education. Very often, only those performers who have got as far as music college or university (and by no means all of those) have been exposed to ideas about period performance. And there have been few books presenting reliable information about the interpretation of the music of the past in a general, non-specialist way.

That is the gap we hope to fill with this series of three guides to the performance of music of different periods: the Baroque period roughly defined as from about 1600 to 1759 (the death of Handel); the Classical from 1759 (Haydn's first symphony) to 1828 (the death of Schubert); the Romantic from 1828 (the composition of Berlioz's Op. 1) to about 1914. The guides are aimed broadly at the Associated Board's own constituency of students (especially at the higher grades) and their teachers – not to mention examiners! But they are not designed as companions to specific exam syllabuses, present or future; and we hope they will be useful to all musicians, including adult amateurs and indeed professionals.

The three volumes all have the same plan. An introductory chapter sketches the historical background to the music of the period; a closing chapter discusses sources and editions. The writers of these, all leading experts in their fields, have taken distinctly different approaches to their tasks, so that the three volumes together offer an introduction to different ways of treating music history and musicology.

In between, each volume has an important general chapter on how the music on the page would have been interpreted by performers at the time, followed by a series of more specialized chapters devoted to keyboard, string and wind instruments and singing. All these are written by musicians who have not only scholarly expertise but also practical experience of performing, often at the highest level. One important point which emerges from these chapters is that different kinds of musicians have always learned from each other. We hope you will read all the chapters, not just those devoted to your own speciality; and also that you will gain enlightenment and stimulation from all the tracks on the accompanying CD.

Another important point which the contributors make many times over is that the task of the performer is not simply to give the most accurate account possible of the notes on the printed page. This is an ideal which has been in circulation only for a very few years in the later twentieth century. In general, for centuries, the performer has been expected to bring his or her own skill and taste to bear on the composer's conception – and in some periods to make a very substantial contribution. So we hope you will treat these guides not as a set of instructions telling you how to achieve a 'correct' interpretation, but as a source of the information you will need in order to give a stylish performance – a collaboration between the composer's inspiration in the past and your own imagination and fantasy in the present.

Christopher Hogwood

Introduction

In one of his most maddeningly cautionary tales, Jorge Luis Borges tells the parable of a minor nineteenth-century French writer, Pierre Menard, who was so besotted with the story of *Don Quixote* that he tried to turn himself into Cervantes – to learn Spanish, become Catholic, fight the Turk, forget three centuries of history – and eventually managed to write again (rather than transcribe) parts of this epic. But, Borges points out, a passage written in the nineteenth century carries a quite different message from the identical words written in 1602.

It is important for 'early' musicians to remember that we can never *be* the past; the significance of what we do depends on the fact that performing is present-tense – although much of our repertoire carries its past with it like DNA, to be ferreted out and acknowledged.

Thirty years ago the buzz words of people doing this ferreting were 'authentic', 'original instruments', 'as-Bach-would-have-heard-it', and so on. Then Andrew Porter devised HIP ('Historically Informed Performance') as a more useful terminology that opened such pursuits to all musicians with a sympathetic mind-set, not simply the 'antiquarians' (of whom I was one!). Some people, misunderstanding the problem, asked why we did not dress in original costumes; one famous conductor even insinuated that we must prefer seventeenth-century plumbing and sanitation. But HIP is not a charade, it is always a modern event that calls for your curiosity and constant questioning.

In this volume, Clifford Bartlett warns against spurious Urtext editions: ask a few pertinent questions before you waste your money – but always take the risk and ask, whatever the context. If that note in Bach sounds odd, query it; if that tempo or dynamic in Purcell or Marini causes raised eyebrows, investigate. And this is a matter for eyes as well as ears. Those paintings showing keyboard instruments being played with their lids closed, or three musicians sharing a part, or horn players holding their instruments vertically: they were not painted by Martians, they are eyewitness accounts.

Many questions have not yet been satisfactorily answered, so you may find yourself a pioneer: ask about early rehearsal methods, the layout of a Baroque orchestra, or the etiquette for accommodating extempore cadenzas in an aria, and you may have to consult history direct. How exactly did they rehearse without bar numbers and pencils and bowing marks? When was the first time a conductor interposed himself between soloist and orchestra in a concerto? Why did ∿ mean one thing in England in 1700, another in 1750 and yet another in 1800?

Codes change meaning with both time and country; and, of course, theories change too, which is good reason for the modern player to avoid permanence: don't write too much down! Memory is developable, and without the permanence of writing you will be able to start fresh again next time. In any case, new theories spring up as fast in musicology as they do in medicine, so your next year's solution may be quite different.

We are not the first people to face the challenge of 'Ancient Musick': Arthur Bedford in 1711 worried about early songs being performed too slowly ('drawling them full as slow again as they were originally intended'), and Mendelssohn had a row in 1845 when he insisted on publishing Handel in Urtext ('on no account whatever would I interpolate marks of expression, *tempi*, etc., or anything else in a score of Handel's, if there is to be any doubt whether they are mine or his').

Better a strong performance fuelled by your personal HIP conviction (even if you change your mind a month later) than a weak one coasting along on received opinion.

This book will, I hope, stimulate but not satisfy your necessary curiosity.

George Pratt

Historical Background

Exploring a distant period

An artistic 'period' cannot be dated precisely. There are always early signs of approaching new ideas, and influences linger beyond the death of a composer or a change in political, social or economic circumstances. There are, though, good reasons for identifying 1600 as a watershed, in Italy at least, with the birth of opera. A century and a half later, Handel's death in 1759 marked the passing of the second giant of the late Baroque, after J. S. Bach.

Looking back 400 years can lead to a compressed, wrong-end-of-tele-scope view. Bear in mind, therefore, that if the Baroque period were ending now, in the early years of the new millennium, it would have begun around 1840. At that point Beethoven and Schubert had died just over a decade ago, and Tchaikovsky was a newborn babe in arms.

The span of time from the mid-nineteenth century to the present day has accommodated enormous changes. Similarly, while some distinctive features unite it, the Baroque period encompasses a huge range of changing musical styles in composition and in performance practice, and of audiences for whom the music was designed.

This chapter is intended, therefore, to outline the distinctive features not only of various places, people and genres of music, but also of an extended period – 160 years – of influences, change and development.

Another misconception can arise from an unconscious assumption that, as music changes, it also becomes more sophisticated, that it improves. But a moment's reflection will remind us that a piece from Claudio Monteverdi's fifth book of madrigals of 1605 is as perfect for its purpose and setting – the court of Mantua in northern Italy – as is a chorus from George Frideric Handel's oratorio *Jephtha* for the Covent Garden theatre in 1752.

A misshapen pearl

The Portuguese used the word *barroco* to describe a flawed pearl. The French version, *baroque*, continued throughout the eighteenth century to imply the bizarre or grotesque. Jean-Jacques Rousseau wrote in his *Dictionnaire de musique* (1768): 'A baroque music is that in which the harmony is confused, charged with modulations and dissonances, the melody is harsh and little natural, the intonation difficult, and the movement constrained'. Only during the twentieth century did the term take on its implications of bold, decorative, confident and flamboyant. This certainly describes the underlying spirit of the age, despite the rich variety of styles throughout the 160 years we are exploring.

Common ground

As well as a vibrant spirit, there are other features which are common throughout Baroque music. The most consistent is the presence of a basso continuo, a line constructed from whichever notes happen to be the lowest sounding at any one time. The implications of this are critical to an understanding of how Baroque composers thought about their music. Listen to a movement from a Mass by Palestrina or Lassus, composers of the high Renaissance. Here the separate lines flow horizontally, in interwoven melodies. They create vertical harmony, of course, but their principal role is melodic. In place of this web of counterpoint, Baroque composers constructed harmony, clearly identifiable chords, which they then used in progressions, horizontally, through a time continuum. Exx. 1.1 and 1.2 show respectively the horizontal flow of counterpoint and the progression of vertical harmony.

Once a composer was thinking vertically, he (rarely 'she' in the Baroque period, though there are a few exceptions) could use dissonance in highly charged and expressive ways. The impact of Orfeo hearing that his new bride has been killed, poisoned by a venomous snake, could move its audience to tears.

Music founded on a clearly defined bass line puts a comparable emphasis on the melody above. The outer parts become polarized. Indeed in Ex. 1.2 Claudio Monteverdi (1567–1643) wrote only Orfeo's vocal line and the bass part. The harmonies are to be filled in by chordal instruments – harpsichord, organ, lute, chitarrone (a long-necked bass lute) or harp – and

Ex. 1.1.
G. P. Palestrina, *Missa terzia* 'Jesu, nostra redemptio' (1582): Kyrie, bb. 1–13. The first entries for each voice are in imitation at various distances: bass and alto within a bar, soprano delayed to b. 4½ and tenor to b. 6, back on the first beat. The second imitative melodic figure or 'point' then begins immediately and less strictly: only the three-crotchet rhythm of 'Ky-rie e-' is consistent. The harmony, while highly controlled, is a by-product of the horizontal melodic lines.

extemporized by the players, guided only by a few figures beneath the bass as a musical shorthand indicating what harmonies are required. Details of how chords are laid out, how many notes are in them, how passing notes might decorate progressions from one to the next – all these are the performer's responsibility.

The continuo tradition lasts throughout the Baroque. A Bach aria or a movement of an instrumental sonata by Handel still requires a player of keyboard or plucked stringed instrument to fill in the harmony between the polarized bass and melody parts. Performers need to be aware that an accompanist, sometimes a soloist, will often be playing editorial additions to the composer's written melody and bass, rather than original notes. (See Chapter 3 'Keyboard', pp. 57–9.)

Another area of common ground throughout the Baroque is the rhetorical power of music. Much of it reaches out to communicate strong passions, persuasive emotions. *The New Grove Dictionary of Music and Musicians* provides a fascinating list, under 'Rhetoric and music', of sixty-one figures with specific rhetorical meaning. Obvious examples are an

Ex. 1.2.
C. Monteverdi, *Orfeo* (1607): Act II, 'Tu se' morta', bb. 312–21 (with editorial right-hand part). Here, the concept is vertical: Orfeo's opening phrase includes a leap to a wholly unprepared crashing dissonance, F♯ above G. Many similar clashes follow, as the singer is overwhelmed with grief at the death of his new wife.

upward leap of exclamation, a rising scale to indicate a question, a falling chromatic scale of sadness. Ex. 1.2 is saturated in rhetorical devices: Orfeo's silence of disbelief at the start; the dissonances already identified on specific poignant words or syllables; the accelerating note values as realization dawns; the rising line to a climax on 'rimano'; the pun on the last syllable, 'no, no'.

Such musical rhetoric was a way of arousing specific passions – fear, love, hatred, anger, joy. The music was – and still is – meant to move us intensely. This has clear implications for us as performers, as also does the convention, in the later Baroque, that any one aria or instrumental movement will normally focus on a single one of the passions, or 'affects' as they were called. Once a mood is established, it will generally be sustained throughout the movement.

Thirdly, Baroque music is steeped in rhythmic vitality. Monteverdi's *Orfeo* includes dance music, which performers would have expected to dance to on stage. Over a hundred years later, in 1727, Bach ended his *St Matthew Passion* with a slow sarabande to convey both lamentation and the promise of redemption as Christ's body is laid to rest.

While powerfully driven rhythms characterize much of Baroque music, polarized melody and rhetorical passion belong above all to dramatic vocal music, and it was here that the new music of the Baroque really began – in Italy.

Italian origins

In 1600 Italy was not the single state it is today. It consisted of separate duchies ruled over by powerful noble families such as the Gonzagas of Mantua, of kingdoms belonging to other countries – Spain ruled Naples until 1713 – and of a swathe of papal states across the middle of the country from Rome in the west to Ferrara in the north-east. Despite this political fragmentation, Italy was united by its common language and by its allegiance to the Pope. Its rulers vied with each other in demonstrating their importance and magnificence with sumptuous palaces, spectacular social events, plays and music.

The invention of opera

In an age of humanism, where man could decide his own destiny rather than leave it wholly in the hands of God, the philosophy and culture of classical Greece was idealized. The Orpheus story, the subject of the first great opera by Monteverdi, is a Greek legend; it opens in the fields of Thrace populated by nymphs and shepherds, a pastoral setting providing escape from the mannered formality of courtly life. It incorporates dances, songs, instrumental music and choruses of rejoicing and dismay. But none of these is a suitable vehicle for conveying dramatic dialogue and narrative. For this, Monteverdi turned to recitative – speaking in music – newly invented by a group of intellectuals, noblemen, poets, musicians, philosophers, in Florence who called themselves the Camerata. The implications of recitative are very significant. As Ex. 1.2 has shown, the bass part moves slowly, and is stable enough for the ear to comprehend highly charged dissonances above it.

Madrigals

Another related stylistic innovation had appeared two years before *Orfeo* in Monteverdi's fifth book of madrigals. The first thirteen pieces are for the customary five unaccompanied voices, but the last six surprisingly require the addition of basso continuo; sections in them for solo voice would be quite incomplete without this instrumental harmonic support. Monteverdi himself described his daring use of dissonance, rationalized by the vertical approach to harmony, as the *seconda pratica*, the second, modern way of writing, compared with the *prima pratica* of interwoven, horizontal counterpoint which controls and restrains its resulting harmony.

Instrumental forces

While courts and major churches employed their own instrumentalists, the idea of a standard orchestra was unknown. For the private performance of *Orfeo* in a room of the ducal palace in Mantua, forty assorted instruments were available and Monteverdi made careful use of them for specific effects. An example is the change to organ with wooden pipes with a chitarrone to accompany Orfeo's cry of anguish (Ex. 1.2). By contrast, Monteverdi's *L'incoronazione di Poppea* (The Coronation of Poppea) was written for public performance in 1642–3 in Venice, in an opera house where, as now, management worked under severe economic constraints. It uses no more than a handful of strings, continuo instruments, and a pair of wind instruments brought in for the magnificent coronation scene shortly before the end. Nor is a costly chorus required. By now, the chief attraction for audiences was solo singing: in recitative for unfolding the action of the plot, and in arias – songs in which the drama pauses and the music holds sway.

Sacred drama

Many characteristics of the new opera found their way into sacred music, particularly oratorio. The Roman composer Giacomo Carissimi (1605–74) wrote *Jephte* in the 1640s – not long after *Poppea*. Like *Orfeo*, it deals with tragedy: Jephtha has inadvertently committed himself to sacrificing his own daughter. Her poignant lament at her approaching death is made up of free recitative interspersed with measured passages of song. Though it was not staged or acted, its mix of recitative and arias looks very like the score of an opera. Only the addition of a narrator to tell the story (as Bach's Evangelist later describes Christ's Passion), and of a chorus, distinguishes it from opera, on paper at least.

Venetian church music

Another influential development in early Baroque music was centred on Venice with its magnificent churches such as the great Basilica of St Mark's, still the centre of tourist attraction today. Within its huge gold-leafed cupolas, singers and instrumentalists performed, sometimes in divided choirs (*cori spezzati*), throwing sound from one side to another in wonderful stereophony. An example of this is *Omnes gentes*, a huge setting of Psalm 47 by Giovanni Gabrieli (*c*.1554-7–1612) for sixteen parts, voices and instruments, in four separate choirs. Together with contrasting sound in space came the notion of dynamic contrast. A justly well-known piece by

Gabrieli is for cornetts (woodwind instruments, fingered like a recorder but blown through a trumpet-like mouthpiece), sackbuts (narrow-bore trombones) and a viola, and derives its title, *Sonata pian'e forte*, from its dramatic use of contrasting loud and quiet sections. This was to have a strong influence on music across the Alps as German composers (most notably Heinrich Schütz) came to admire and imitate Venetian church music.

Instrumental music

Although it will be clear by now that vocal music, especially solo song, was the dominant music in Italy, instrumental music was not unimportant. The seventeenth century saw the growth of the Italian violin-making tradition centred on Cremona. The Amati family had worked there since the middle of the sixteenth century, and its most famous member, Nicolò Amati (1596–1684), taught Antonio Stradivari (1644-9–1737) the craft with which he created what remain the world's most treasured string instruments. The solo music for violin from this period is still relatively little known, though you will find recordings of composers such as Biagio Marini (1594–1663). His sonatas (from *suonari* – to sound as opposed to sing) are in several short linked sections rather than extended movements, their harmony less purposeful than the forceful drive of, say, Vivaldi or Telemann, in the following century. Again, though, they demonstrate the interest in solo music, in polarized top and bottom parts, filled up with continuo improvisation in between. If you can find a recording of this music, you will hear clearly that it is idiomatic: it could not be played successfully on any instrument other than the violin. This was a developing trend during the Baroque, so that Bach, at the end of the period, could consciously exchange idioms, for example asking a voice to imitate characteristic writing for trumpet in the final 'Alleluia' of Cantata No. 51.

Sonatas such as Marini's have two polarized lines, top and bottom. Another very common texture has three lines, two on top and a bass: the trio sonata, most often for two violins and continuo. Purcell, later in the Baroque, was careful to stress that each part 'has as much predominancy as the other': they are of equal importance.

Keyboard music

Keyboard music in Italy was heard in chamber and church. The former was the preserve of the privileged and wealthy, but everyone could hear music in church as part of the weekly High Mass. In Rome, the most famous and influential composer was Girolamo Alessandro Frescobaldi (1583–1643). His keyboard music includes canzonas, pieces that start with a characteristic 'long-short-short' rhythm; ricercars, beginning with a single line and then building towards a complex contrapuntal texture; toccatas, 'touch pieces', demonstrating the virtuosity of florid figuration; and *intonazioni*, 'intonations', designed to provide the church choir with their starting note before they sing, and often alternating with sections of music for organ alone.

Keyboard music and keyboard instruments give us a fascinating clue about how acutely sensitive were performers, and presumably their audiences too, to tuning and sonority. The sustained sound of the organ demonstrates vividly the character of the unequal temperaments to which instruments were tuned. To explain this briefly, if you tune precisely 3rds one above the other – C–E, E–G♯, G♯–B♯ – the resulting apparent 'octave' is wildly flat. But the perfectly tuned 3rds of 'mean-tone temperament' create, in less remote keys, a warmth and sonority which we simply cannot experience with our present-day compromise 'equal temperament', which irons out the mathematical anomalies inherent in tuning systems. (For more detail, see Chapter 2 'Notation and Interpretation', p. 23.)

Across the Alps to Germany

Italian arts and culture reached out over the whole of Europe. There were strong trading links between wealthy German merchants on the Baltic coast and Venice, gateway to the Mediterranean and to the spices and treasures of the east. But, while Italy was unified by the Catholic faith, Germany was riven by religious strife. The Thirty Years' War (1618–48) between Catholics and Protestants caused terrible loss of life, drained the potential prosperity of the country, and inhibited extravagant musical activity in courts and city states.

Sacred music

Nonetheless, Protestant and Catholic traditions met and overlapped in music, notably in the way in which German composers treated the Lutheran chorale. When Martin Luther led the Reformation at the beginning of the sixteenth century, he had declared music 'to be praised as second only to the Word of God because by it are all the emotions swayed'. It was a powerful force in worship, to be sung by the congregation as well as performed by the professional musicians – choirs, organists, instrumentalists. Luther himself composed chorales, an example being the familiar *Ein feste Burg ist unser Gott* (A safe stronghold our God is still). Chorales have two equally essential elements, music and text. In some cases, composers took both and wove them into magnificent works in the modern Italian style. Recent recordings have revealed just how striking much of this music is. Michael Praetorius (1571–1621) in his collection *Polyhymnia caduceatrix* (The Healing Muse, 1619) alternated and combined as many as five 'choirs' – soloists, ensembles, instrumentalists – in the grandest Venetian-style stereophony, but often basing the whole of a piece on both the words and the melody of a chorale.

Luther's advocacy of music ensured that the towns of Protestant north Germany had fine organs in their churches, and well-respected posts for their Kantors, or directors of music, whose functions normally included playing the organ, training the choir, providing music for civic occasions, and often teaching in school (the role which J. S. Bach was to fill in Leipzig).

Heinrich Schütz (1585–1672) lived and worked in the court at Dresden, where Praetorius visited him. The connection between the Venetian style and the music of Schütz is even more explicit as he visited Venice twice in his life, once to be a pupil of Gabrieli and later meeting Monteverdi. Schütz's *Christmas History*, published in 1664, provides fascinating evidence of the continuing tradition between Monteverdi early in the Baroque and J. S. Bach a hundred years later. As you can readily hear from a recording, the story is told through an Evangelist, singing recitative, generally above a simple continuo, though passionate chromaticism such as describes 'lamentation, weeping and mourning' matches the rhetorical force of Monteverdi. Characters sing their roles: a trio of three Wise Men; Herod, accompanied by a Venetian-sounding brass ensemble; angels, associated with string instruments. Choruses at the beginning and end frame the whole work, which has much in common with Bach's dramatic music some sixty years later, especially the St John and St Matthew Passions.

Instrumental music

Although some German courts imported Italian opera, it was not the dominant genre that it was in Italy. Germans, and Bohemians to the east of them, had a strong partiality for instrumental music, and most major towns employed a band of wind players to provide music for municipal occasions and for dance. German composers matched Italians in striving at all costs to make their music expressive, to touch the hearts as well as the minds of listeners. A striking example was the Bohemian violinist and composer Heinrich Ignaz Franz von Biber (1644–1704). He wrote some of the most difficult music of this period that a string player is ever likely to encounter. He made great use of *scordatura*, i.e. unconventional tunings of the violin strings, to create strikingly unusual colours (see Chapter 4 'Strings', p. 80). Such music demonstrates clearly that, as in Italy so too in Germany, Baroque music was intended to arouse the passions and communicate its emotions vividly.

Although courts and the larger ecclesiastical foundations customarily had a nucleus of string instrumentalists with the town wind players close at hand, the modern orchestra grew up first in the court of the King of France.

Westwards to France

French Baroque music is highly distinctive. Here alone in Europe, Italian music largely failed to infiltrate, and a series of unique factors combined to create an unmistakable national style.

First, the kings of France wielded absolute power. Louis XIV, the 'Sun King', could, and did, bestow on his most favoured subjects quite extraordinary privileges. For example, Jean-Baptiste Lully (1632–87) was given a monopoly on sung drama: for some time, nowhere in France could more than two singers and six instrumentalists perform it except within Lully's Académie Royale de Musique, a company which he had acquired with the King's approval and support. Words and music were devised to flatter the King, and he himself took part in many of the sumptuous entertainments in Paris and, from 1683, in his magnificent palace at Versailles, the envy of courts throughout the whole of Europe.

Dramatic music

The French have always taken their language very seriously. Indeed, the Académie Française was founded in 1635 to protect its purity (and even today there are regular attempts to purge the language of foreign additions such as 'le week-end'). There was a strong tradition of spoken drama, so opera, sung and in a foreign language, had little appeal for the French. During the first half of the seventeenth century, attempts to introduce

Italian opera failed, and instead France acquired a wholly distinctive kind of musical drama. It was effectively invented by Lully (surprisingly, an Italian by birth, but a clever schemer who took French citizenship and a French wife). He radically changed the nature of recitative in his *tragédies lyriques* (not Italian 'operas') by responding to the stresses and inflections of French using precise note values and varying time signatures. In place of extended arias, this music incorporates simple airs with short, regular phrases, often repeated and so instantly memorable. A characteristic of such French music, essential for the performer to recognize and phrase correctly, is the 'feminine ending', the strong–weak stress pattern used in poetic French: 'je vous *aim*-e'.

Dance

Dance too was central to courtly entertainment in France. The King himself danced major roles in *divertissements*, the staged performances with lavish scenery incorporating machines that allowed chariots to descend from the heavens, clouds to open up and reveal musicians sitting within them – spectacles which delighted and amazed their audiences much as do the computer graphics of today's television technology. So French music is saturated in dance rhythms – as in a suite with allemande, courante (subtly alternating between simple 3/2 and compound 6/4 time) and menuet. Again, performers need to reflect that much of this music was actually intended for dancing to, and even in concert performance its metre needs to be appropriately stable and regular.

Orchestral developments

One highly influential outcome of Lully's position at the French court was his contribution to the birth of the regular orchestra, playing with professional unanimity and discipline. Louis XIV surrounded himself with music, as he rose, as he went to bed, while he ate. During worship he preferred the spoken Low Mass, when he could listen to a *grand motet* for a *petit choeur* of soloists, a *grand choeur* and a large instrumental ensemble, performed above the liturgy muttered inaudibly by the priest. Publicly, too, music provided a background to every social event and diversion. There were over 150 musicians employed at the French court, including the *Vingt-quatre violons du Roi*, the King's 'twenty-four violins' (i.e. string players). Their music was laid out in five parts: violins, three viola lines and basses, a rich texture which also characterizes French choral music for both church and stage. To the strings could be added wind players from the *écurie* (literally the 'stables'), musicians who played for outdoor events such as hunting parties and military ceremonies. Lully imposed on his core of players a level of orchestral discipline hitherto unknown, including unanimous bowing and the level of crisp ensemble which is essential to play the sharply dotted rhythms of the slow first section of a French 'ouverture' such as opened Lully's stage works. Another rhythmic feature of French music was that of *notes inégales*, unequal notes. Although these are notated as pairs of equal quavers, there is clear evidence that they are intended to be played with a lilting inequality, all too easily overlooked by performers today. (See Chapter 2 'Notation and Interpretation', pp. 36–42.)

Lute and keyboard

An immensely popular instrument in France was the lute. The limitations of playing such an instrument, with only one hand available to stop the strings while the other is occupied in plucking them, created a distinctive style of music. It is difficult to carry on extended counterpoint on lute, chitarrone or guitar, so it was often implied by false 'voice-leading': one part starting its line but dropping out to allow subsequent 'voices' to follow it in imitation. The *style brisé*, 'broken style', has harmonies built in arpeggio patterns of notes from different registers, as best fit under the hands. Above all, the short-lived tone of the lute was decorated and extended by ornamentation. These characteristics became so much part of the musical language in general that they infused French music of all kinds. François Couperin (1668–1733) carefully listed and explained exactly how the signs for such ornaments in his harpsichord music should be interpreted (see Chapter 2 'Notation and Interpretation', Ex. 2.18, p. 44). Then (as now) they were not optional: Couperin himself complained that to omit them was 'unpardonable negligence'. Similarly, French vocal *airs*, so simple-looking on paper, invite and require much delicate embellishment in performance.

Late Baroque

Though Lully died in 1687 (of gangrene, having hit his toe with a sharp cane while conducting a performance celebrating the King's recovery from an operation), his individual style remained the standard by which all other French music for stage and orchestra was judged, until the first stage work of Jean-Philippe Rameau (1683–1764): *Hippolyte et Aricie*, a *tragédie lyrique*. Although the French public immediately divided itself into two opposing camps, the 'Lullistes' and the 'Ramoneurs' (a pun on the French word for 'chimney-sweeps'), Rameau absorbed the subtlety of Lully's recitative and his orchestral discipline. He added, however, a particular sensitivity to instrumental colour. A recording of his opera *Castor et Pollux* will repay listening to, above all for the overwhelmingly beautiful *air* 'Tristes apprêts', in which Télaïre mourns the death of her beloved Castor, accompanied by the plangent sound of strings and a solo bassoon.

Across the Channel to England

The present-day road map of France still reflects the Paris-centred nature of the country since before the seventeenth and eighteenth centuries. Very little music of significance was available outside the capital and neighbouring Versailles. Music in England was similarly centred on London, but the political constitution could hardly have been more different. It took a revolution in France to bring down the monarchy at the end of the eighteenth century; it took only a decision of Parliament to decide that Charles I should be beheaded, and the monarchy suspended for the eleven years of the Commonwealth (1649–60).

The restoration of the monarchy

English Baroque music is a fascinating mix of native tradition and influences from abroad. It developed late, however. Modern Italian basso continuo was not common until well into the 1630s, the Puritans banned public music in church and theatre, and it was not until the restoration of the monarchy that music was restored in church and court. The new king, Charles II, was described by a contemporary diarist as 'a light and airy prince'. He had spent his exile in France, and brought to England a passion for all things French. He established a band of string players in imitation of the *Vingt-quatre violons du Roi* of Louis XIV – the 'four-and-twenty black-birds' of the nursery rhyme. They played not only in courtly entertain-ments, most notably masques (including dancing and singing), but also during church services in the Chapel Royal. There had been a tradition of 'verse-anthems' – solos, ensembles and recurring choral sections, accom-panied by a consort of viols or other instruments – from the early years of the seventeenth century. Now, such anthems provided the opportunity for long opening ritornellos played by five-part modern strings, and continued with Italianate solo declamation, but with a Lullian sensitivity to descript-ive word-setting. Indeed, the King had sent a young English composer, Pelham Humfrey (1647/8–74), to Paris to learn the French style from Lully himself, and he returned, we are told, 'an absolute Monsieur'. Humfrey's anthems have been recorded, and listening to one will bring vividly to life the combination of French rhythms and sonorities, Italian declamation,

Ex. 1.3. H. Purcell, Burial Service, second version *c*.1679–81: 'Man that is born of a woman', bb. 6–12. Many weak-beat crotchet chords are dissonant. In b. 3, the alto *ab* lends a plain-tive quality to an expected tonic chord. Bar 5 introduces a flattened leading note (*bb* in the bass), creating false rela-tions with the B♮s before and after. The example ends with a spine-chilling 'English cadence'; juxtaposing *db'* and *d♮'*.

and the tone and language of the English cathedral choir tradition. A further uniquely English characteristic lies in the harmonic dissonances.

Henry Purcell

This harmonic piquancy is a defining characteristic of the music of England's arguably greatest composer, Henry Purcell (1659–95). (For a characteristic example, see Ex. 1.3.)

In Purcell's theatre music you also find strong French and Italian traits. *The Fairy Queen* (first performance 1692) is a semi-opera, a spoken play based on Shakespeare's *A Midsummer Night's Dream*, with extended musical interludes. There are many dances in the French idiom, while some of the songs are full-blown da capo arias in the latest Italian manner (see below). The musical interludes in *The Fairy Queen* include lively humour – a drunken poet, a rustic courtship – and some exquisitely beautiful songs including 'O let me weep', a 'plaint' for soprano, duetting with a solo oboe, which begins over the repeating pattern of a 'ground bass'. The ground bass was a common Baroque structural device, the best-known example perhaps being Dido's lament, the last air of Purcell's only opera, *Dido and Aeneas* (1689 or earlier).

Italy again – vocal and instrumental music

Opera

During the latter years of the seventeenth century, Italian opera reached unparalleled heights of popularity, with public audiences still filling theatres not only in Venice but also in Rome and Naples, where Alessandro Scarlatti (1660–1725) proved to be the most influential opera composer of his day. Neapolitan commercial *opera seria* ('serious' opera, purged of comic episodes and confusing changes of time and place) is based on heroic characters, either from myth or history, engaged in conflicts above all between love and duty – noble sentiments with which the audience could identify. It virtually never uses a chorus, which was considered too expensive, and requires a nucleus of orchestral strings and continuo, with occasional oboes or flutes and, for celebratory occasions, trumpets. And it focuses wholly on solo singers and their arias. In time, the form became highly stylized. Recitative became more perfunctory, a vehicle for fast action and dialogue, to be sung at half-voice and with rhythmic freedom to forward the dramatic action rather than to demonstrate the vocal qualities of the singer. The aria, on the other hand, grew into a large-scale, dramatically static display piece, almost always in da capo form. The first section is sung virtually unadorned; the middle section is contrasted in key and, often, in instrumentation; finally the first section returns, but so decorated by the singer that it builds, often thrillingly, on the simple first hearing. Though *opera seria* differs from recitative-based early opera, the intention to move the emotions remains in full measure. Each aria normally remains (at least in its outer sections) in one mood or 'affect', be it a vibrant call to arms or a passionate plaint of unrequited love; and the vocal display, the purposeful harmony, and the focus on the solo singer (occasionally a pair of duetting lovers) make this some of the most powerful vocal music in the whole repertoire.

Fig. 1.1. Interior of the Teatro Regio, Turin, by Pietro Domenico Olivero, *c*.1740.

Concerto and sonata

The relationship between voice and accompaniment in opera arias resembles that between soloist and orchestra in instrumental concertos. The notion of contrast – loud/quiet, few/many performers, sound to the left/to the right – has always been a favourite device of composers. Gabrieli's divided choirs in Venice, as the seventeenth century began, are a clear example. From 1681 onwards Arcangelo Corelli (1653–1713) published sets of string trio sonatas, some for use in church, the rest for chamber performance. They are in short but quite distinct movements compared with the continuous sections of earlier instrumental sonatas. Like those of earlier Italian composers, these 'trio' sonatas actually use four players: two violins, and a continuo section of (for example) cello and harpsichord. Corelli also wrote similar pieces but designated sections of them to be played by full string orchestra, alternating with the solo quartet. This is the principle of his concerti grossi Op. 6, written probably during the 1680s but not published until 1714. They work as trio sonatas if the full forces are not available, but they were performed at times 'with the greatest exactitude by a large number of players', suggesting that Lully's contributions to orchestral discipline had reached Italy.

It was normal still for composers to depend on patrons for their employment. Corelli's first major appointment was in the service of the exiled Queen Christina of Sweden. Later, senior members of the ecclesiastical

Fig. 1.2. Christofer Schor, *Festival in the Piazza di Spagna*, Rome, 1687, showing a large orchestra playing outdoors in Rome, possibly directed from the violin by Corelli.

aristocracy, Cardinals Pamphili and Ottoboni, employed him in their palaces. You can still visit Ottoboni's palace, the Cancelleria, in Rome, and there see the church of San Lorenzo in Damaso, where Corelli's church sonatas and concertos were first played during the course of the Mass.

Venice provided secure employment of a different kind, most notably for Antonio Vivaldi (1678–1741). He worked for much of his life as director of music at the Pio Ospedale della Pietà, one of four orphanages in Venice. Here, in a city-state with a tradition of providing social services to support unwanted children, music was central to the curriculum, and Vivaldi clearly had many talented young players of every conceivable instrument. Much of his output of over 500 concertos is for solo instrument, most often his own, the violin; but other concertos, solo or multiple, feature the rarer colours of the mandolin, chalumeau (a wonderfully dark-sounding precursor of the clarinet), viola d'amore, sopranino recorder and so on: no instrument is unprovided for, though there is very little for the keyboard, for which Bach was the first significant composer of concertos.

While Corelli's concerti grossi were in several movements, and some of them in turn included sections in different tempos creating a variable patchwork rather than a predictable order, Vivaldi's concertos are mostly in a standard three-movement form – fast–slow–fast – which has remained the norm for concertos right through to the present day. The outer move-

ments are strongly shaped in what is often called 'tutti-ritornello' form: the full orchestra (or *tutti*), playing different versions of its opening statement (called *ritornelli*, or 'little returns'), alternates with brilliant episodes for the soloist or soloists. This form permeated a great deal of later Baroque music, beyond concertos: thousands of opera arias owe much to it, as instruments first introduce the voice, then alternate with it.

The girls of the Venetian orphanage played and sang in the Church of the Pietà where visitors, from all over Europe, would shuffle their feet and blow their noses to show their appreciation in a context where conventional applause would have been unacceptable.

Handel – in England

George Frideric Handel (1685–1759) was above all an opera composer, learning in the orchestral pit of the opera at Hamburg in northern Germany, then in Italy – Florence, Rome, Venice and Naples. In London, from 1710, he was commissioned by theatre directors to write Italian operas, and later took on the role of impresario, hiring the King's Theatre and financing productions himself. This independence of employment, if not of patronage, was virtually unique in the Baroque, and is testimony to Handel's strength of purpose and his outstanding reputation then, as now.

His audiences in England consisted of royalty, the nobility and the public. The better-off took boxes for the whole season, since an evening at the opera was a major social event. They experienced a highly stylized musical drama, reading by candlelight a translation of the Italian libretto, paying little attention to the recitatives, but listening with rapt attention to the arias sung by the star soloists. Newspaper reports and personal letters refer not to characters and their roles in the plot, but to actual singers: they held the stage, with little or no action around them, and each aria led to an exit, allowing singers to return for rapturous applause. Particularly admired were the castratos, who had voices of boy sopranos or altos yet the maturity and power of full-grown men, a sound which is now lost to us. They were received like the pop stars of today.

Yet Handel had a strong dramatic vision, and his music generously repays being projected with a clear understanding of its original dramatic context. This is true not only of his operas but also of his oratorios, to which he turned as Italian opera began to fall out of favour. Most recreate

Fig. 1.3. Stage of the King's Theatre, Haymarket, London, anon., *c.*1725.

dramatic Old Testament stories, adapted into librettos in English, developing the same conflicts – between love and honour, between good and evil – that characterized Italian opera. (*Messiah*, often assumed to be the paradigm, is totally different from any other of his oratorios in every respect.) They were performed in the theatre, without scenery and action, though Handel occasionally reveals his imaginary vision of the action by inserting stage directions.

Oratorios were sung from scores rather than memory; and so a chorus, normally too expensive to rehearse in opera but a popular element of the English musical tradition, became an economic proposition – and often a major element.

Much of Handel's other music is also related to his dramatic works: for example, his organ concertos were written for himself to play between the acts of oratorios.

Bach, and the late Baroque in Germany

While Handel developed a foreign genre, Italian opera, to extinction, and invented English dramatic oratorio to replace it, the music of Johann Sebastian Bach (1685–1750) is a remarkable synthesis of styles from throughout Europe.

For all but six years of his mature working life, Bach was an organist. His reputation rested far more on his playing than on his composing. He lived in a country still divided by faith, Lutherans to the north, Catholics to the south. Its courts were many, varied, and often intensely competitive. They aped French manners and the flamboyance and music of Versailles; they imported Italian opera and instrumental music. Bach's originality rests on his integration of these elements from abroad with the contrapuntal bent of a devout Lutheran church organist, all controlled by craftsmanship the like of which the world has perhaps never seen, before or since.

The largest part of his output was of cantatas, some 200 extant, many more lost. It is important for performers to recognize that these were conceived 'like a piece from an opera, composed of recitative style and arias' (the words of the librettist of many cantatas, Pastor Neumeister of Hamburg). The two extant Passions, based on the gospels of St John and St Matthew, add an Evangelist to narrate the story, together with specified characters including Jesus. Arias transfigure, though still reflect, their secular models. In Cantata No. 80, *Ein feste Burg ist unser Gott*, a swaggering bass accompanied by vigorous violins sings of victory, while sopranos add the chorale melody and text, phrase by phrase, above; a soprano cries out for her heart's desire, Jesus; the alto and tenor duet in 3rds and in close imitation, like a pair of lovers reconciled. The opening movement is a fugue, based on a chorale, structured on the tutti-ritornello form of Vivaldi's concertos, a striking example of Bach's ability to synthesize the various influences around him. A plain, four-part chorale harmonization ends most cantatas, either sung by the congregation or at least so familiar to them that both words and music would be 'sung' in the mind.

Bach's responsibilities to his church employers required him to provide organ introductions to hymns in the form of chorale preludes. These too borrowed from and enlarged upon models: a free fantasia, a fugue based

Fig. 1.4. A torchlit student concert by the Leipzig Collegium Musicum.

upon each successive line of the chorale, a trio sonata texture with the chorale phrases entering in long notes.

Bach's concertos depend heavily on the Italian models of Vivaldi, but with a more active bass line, denser harmony and the contrapuntal imagination of an organist. As an organist rather than a celebrated singer or virtuoso violinist, he conceived the idea of arranging several concertos for keyboard and orchestra. Much of his solo keyboard music presents suites of dances in the French fashion, and even such seemingly abstract works as the preludes of the forty-eight preludes and fugues (*Das wohltemperirte Clavier*, The Well-Tempered Clavier) have strong dance characteristics.

As well as working, not always contentedly, for church authorities in Weimar and Leipzig, with an intervening period as a court music director, Bach involved himself in public concert promotion, most notably with the Leipzig Collegium Musicum, a body which had been founded in 1702 by Georg Philipp Telemann (1681–1767) and for which Bach provided such secular works as the 'Coffee Cantata' and his French-indebted orchestral suites. The Collegium met in the garden of a Leipzig coffee house in summer, indoors in winter, and provided a platform for young and promising performers.

Telemann was particularly concerned to make music available to the layman with publications such as *Der getreue Music-Meister* (The Faithful Music Master), a weekly journal including sonatas manageable today, as then, by talented amateurs. As well as earning the distinction of being reputedly the most prolific composer Western music has ever known, he marks the close of the Baroque era. The style of his later music is increasingly elegant and *galant* – lightly accompanied, free from the constraints and self-imposed disciplines of counterpoint, written in balanced phrases punctuated by regular cadences.

The function of music was changing, too. Courtly and ecclesiastical patronage remained – and exists still in modern-day sponsorship and national and regional arts funding programmes. But, by 1760, music was becoming increasingly the birthright of the wider middle classes, and its appeal was broadening to take account of their taste as the high Baroque gave way to the orderliness of early Classicism.

Peter Holman

Notation and Interpretation

I am writing this (and you are reading it) because we have a problem. The way music is performed has changed radically over the centuries, just as music itself has changed: performing style is intimately linked to compositional style. So how are we to perform old music now?

One solution, of course, is to modernize it so that it conforms to the performing style of our own time. That can be stimulating, especially when it is done by composers such as Elgar or Peter Maxwell Davies; and it was what J. S. Bach did when he orchestrated a Palestrina mass, and what Mozart did when he re-orchestrated Handel's *Messiah*. But we have increasingly felt uncomfortable with that approach, or simply with relying on a bundle of inherited performing traditions. For better or worse, we have been drawn to the task of trying to perform old music using the instruments, the forces and the performing conventions that the composers themselves used. This can never be a completely successful exercise, and music of the past can never have the same effect on us as it did on those performers and listeners who played it or heard it when it was new, for we are modern people with modern assumptions and expectations. But that does not mean that the task is not worthwhile.

Most of the problems relating to what has come to be called performance practice arise from the way music is notated, or how we misunderstand that notation. This does not mean that old notation was primitive or inaccurate, only that over the centuries composers gradually took over interpretative decisions previously left to the performer. In the Middle Ages composers were expected to specify only the notes and the rhythms. By the sixteenth century they had assumed responsibility for specifying exact text underlay (how the words fitted the notes) and accidentals. By and large, they did not specify particular voices and instruments until the seventeenth century, nor dynamics and expression marks until the eighteenth century. There was no simple way of specifying absolute tempo before the metronome was invented in the early nineteenth century. Thus, if you find 'hairpins' ($<$ $>$), elaborate expression marks or metronome marks in Baroque music they are almost certainly additions made by a later editor; if the edition makes no distinction between them and what the composer wrote, beware! (See Chapter 7, 'Sources and Editions'.)

Incidentally, the label 'Baroque' is misleading, and was applied to music only in the twentieth century. The distinction between 'Renaissance' and 'Baroque' is useful since there were major changes of style and performing conventions around 1600. But it could be argued that 1700 is a more important style boundary than 1750, the conventional end of the Baroque period. Much writing on Baroque performance practice suffers from the tendency to apply the opinions of mid-eighteenth-century writers such as Quantz, Leopold Mozart and C. P. E. Bach to seventeenth-century music; as a result, Schütz and Buxtehude too often sound like J. S. Bach, or Purcell and Blow like Handel.

Instrumentation

We need to bear in mind the stylistic divide around 1700 when we decide which voices or instruments to use. In the early seventeenth century it was still common for composers not to specify particular voices and instruments, and a good deal of flexibility was often expected when they were specified. For instance, violins and cornetts were often given as alternatives for the upper parts of early seventeenth-century sonatas, while bass parts could be allocated to the bass viol (viola da gamba), bass violin (the ancestor of the cello), *fagotto* (early bassoon) or trombone. Similarly, the lute, archlute, theorbo, Baroque guitar, harp, harpsichord and organ were all used as continuo instruments, sometimes in quite large combinations: Matthew Locke's *Broken Consort* suites for two violins and bass (1661) seem to have been performed with a continuo section consisting of three theorboes and organ. Chamber organs were commonly used in secular music all over Europe until about 1700, and in England throughout the Baroque period. We should not assume that continuo lines were always doubled by bowed strings or wind instruments at this period. In sonatas they seem to have been used only when the music included an obbligato bass part (more elaborate than the continuo bass line); and solo vocal music was usually accompanied just by the lute or the theorbo – or in church just by the organ.

Instruments began to be specified more precisely in the late seventeenth century as composers wrote more specifically and idiomatically for them. Each of the main solo instruments used in chamber music, the violin, the recorder, the flute and the oboe, had its own characteristics, which means that it is usually possible to work out which is intended even if none is specified. Sonatas with soprano parts written down to g can only be for violin, as can those that have double stops; music for alto recorder (usually called 'flute', *flûte* or *flauto* at the time) goes down only to f' and tends to be written in flat keys; music for flute (usually called 'German flute', *flûte allemande* or *traverso*), by contrast, is usually in sharp keys, and goes down to d'; music for Baroque oboe is usually written in flat keys, and goes down to c' but avoids $c\sharp'$. Of course, it was common at the time to transpose music to fit different instruments. Some of the recorder repertoire is violin music transposed up a 3rd, and there is no reason why similar transpositions should not be made today. Continuo scoring tended to be much more standardized in the eighteenth century. The normal combination for chamber music was cello and harpsichord, though the bass viol remained popular in France until after 1750, and it was common in Italy to accompany sonatas just with the cello. Conversely, Handel labelled the continuo parts of a number of his solo sonatas simply *cembalo*, perhaps implying that he intended them to be played on the harpsichord without cello or bass viol.

Key associations, temperament and pitch

The limitations of Baroque wind instruments contributed to a series of key associations that have implications for performance practice. For instance, F major was thought to be a pastoral key partly because the recorder, with its associations with shepherds, went down to *f'*, just as the natural trumpet, which was normally in C or D, reinforced the idea that those keys were martial and triumphant. These associations sometimes persisted on other instruments: J. S. Bach's organ Pastorale BWV 590 is in F major, while François Couperin's 'La triomphante' from the *Second livre de pieces de clavecin* (1716–17) is in D major. It has to be said, however, that the systematic lists of key associations set down by Jean Rousseau (1691), Marc-Antoine Charpentier (*c.*1692), Johann Mattheson (1713) and Jean-Philippe Rameau (1722) are too contradictory to provide a blanket guide to the performance of Baroque music, however useful they may be for the music of the individuals concerned.

Another set of associations was created by the unequal temperament used on keyboard instruments. In the early seventeenth century a tuning now known as ¼-comma mean-tone was used, giving beautifully in-tune chords with pure 3rds, but restricting the player to a small group of home keys. All keys are playable in the modified mean-tone used from about 1650 to the early nineteenth century, but the 3rds of the chords become increasingly wide the further you go round the key cycle, or circle of 5ths. This means that each key has a distinct character: F minor has a dissonant subdominant chord (its 3rd, more C♯ than D♭, is very flat), while B minor has a dissonant dominant chord (its 3rd, a B♭ rather than an A♯, is very sharp), and so on. For this reason, Baroque keyboard music should be played in unequal temperament to get its full flavour. If you are playing an equally-tempered instrument, it will help to know that the more extreme keys were often used to intensify musical representations of violence, horror or despair. F minor, for instance, was chosen by Purcell for the witches' scene in *Dido and Aeneas*, and by Handel for 'Surely he hath borne our griefs' and 'And with his stripes' in *Messiah*.

Chromaticism also becomes more expressive in unequal temperament, since the semitones in a chromatic scale are not all the same size, and in ¼-comma mean-tone they vary a good deal: contrary to modern 'expressive' intonation, the sharps are lower than the flats, giving a passage such as Ex. 2.1 a strange and almost bizarre quality. Although temperaments are essential only on chord-playing instruments such as harpsichords, organs and lutes, singers and players of single-line instruments were acutely aware of them throughout the Baroque period. Pier Francesco Tosi, for instance, included a long discussion of major and minor semitones in his influential singing treatise *Opinioni de' cantori antichi e moderni* (1723), best known from John Ernest Galliard's English translation *Observations on the Florid Song* (1742). Incidentally, it is now thought that J. S. Bach's *Das wohltemperirte Clavier* (The Well-Tempered Clavier) was written to exploit a type of unequal temperament rather than equal temperament.

The modern pitch standard, *a'* = 440 Hz, was arrived at only in the last century, and in the last twenty or thirty years another standard, *a'* = 415,

Ex. 2.1. M. Rossi, *Toccate e corenti*, second edition (1657): Toccata No. 7, bb. 72–83.

has developed for the performance of Baroque music with 'original' or 'period' instruments. These terms are in quotation marks here because $a' = 415$ is basically a modern convenience pitch, fixed a semitone below $a' = 440$ so that transposition on harpsichords and organs can be made by using keyboards specially built to slide sideways. Copies of historic wind instruments often have to be modified to fit it. Handel's tuning fork sounds $a' = 422.5$, while wind instruments used in Purcell's London or Lully's Paris play at about $a' = 405$, and pitches as low as $a' = 392$ (a tone below modern pitch) were used in France and Rome. Conversely, the pitch of wind instruments and organs in the sixteenth and early seventeenth centuries was often at least a semitone above $a' = 440$. All this will not concern you directly if you are using modern instruments, though singers may want to transpose up music intended for high pitch, such as German seventeenth-century church music, or to transpose down music intended for the very low French pitch; sometimes you will find that editors have done the job for you. The pitch level can have a crucial bearing on the type of voices used: at $a' = 405$ some of Purcell's 'countertenor' solos are much more suited to high tenors than falsettos.

Notation

The notation of the Baroque period is deceptively similar to our own, and that can be a danger: it is easy to assume that familiar symbols meant the same to people at the time as they do to us. By and large, however, you should not have much problem with the way pitches are notated, though if you are using facsimiles you will often have to contend with various C clefs, and the upper parts of French chamber music sometimes use the so-called French violin clef (G on the bottom line), which can catch out the unwary. One problem is the way accidentals were notated. Sharps usually cancelled flats and vice versa until about 1700, and throughout the Baroque period it is unwise to assume that accidentals last to the end of the bar in the modern way. Also, until the middle of the seventeenth century performers were routinely expected to add accidentals in performance according to the rules of what is loosely called *musica ficta*. Flats are often needed to avoid tritones (augmented 4ths or diminished 5ths), while sharps are needed to raise leading notes in cadences or to avoid a piece ending with a minor final chord. Modern editors usually modernize accidentals, placing the ones they add in small type or over the notes concerned, though I frequently come across editions that do not provide all the accidentals required.

Rhythm is more of a problem. One of the most off-putting aspects of early seventeenth-century notation is the use of a minim beat (or in triple time even a semibreve beat); the modern crotchet beat gradually came in during the century. The problem is made more difficult by our tendency to misunderstand how and why music was written with bar lines. Single parts were not usually barred until after 1650, while scores were nearly always regularly barred, often in two-minim units. Unfortunately, editors often retain these bar lines in modern editions, not understanding that they are there just for alignment and do not imply stresses. This can lead performers to take a piece such as Purcell's three-part Pavan in A minor Z. 749 (Ex. 2.2) at half speed, for they assume that the beat is in crotchets, whereas it is actually in minims, as in earlier pavans. In triple time you will frequently come across hemiolas, the trick of displacing accents across two bars so that they fall **1** 2 **3** / 1 **2** 3 instead of the expected **1** 2 3 / **1** 2 3. They are generally found just before cadences, and should not be heavily stressed. It is usually best to emphasize only the first beat, as in Handel's chorus 'And the glory of the Lord' from *Messiah* (Ex. 2.3), where stressing the second beat of the hemiola produces an inappropriate stress on the word 'be'.

The other main problem is the relationship between different time signatures. Around 1600 the medieval proportional system was still in use, which related all time signatures to a fundamental semibreve pulse or *tactus*. The *tactus* could be marked by rising and falling motions of the

Ex. 2.2. H. Purcell, Pavan in A minor Z. 749, *c.*1677–8: bb. 1–14.

Ex. 2.3. G. F. Handel, *Messiah*, 1741: 'And the glory of the Lord', chorus parts, bb. 34–8.

hand, and was theoretically related to the pulse-rate of a man breathing normally – perhaps 60–70 per minute. According to the system ¢ was twice as fast as c, and ⊙ (or sometimes 2 in seventeenth-century French and English music) was twice as fast as ¢. However, Christopher Simpson wrote in *A Compendium of Practical Musick* (1667) that ¢ 'is properly a sign of Diminution' (i.e. it indicates double speed), though 'many dash it so without any such Intention'. The instructions added to Purcell's *A Choice Collection of Lessons for the Harpsichord or Spinnet* in 1696 just say of c, ¢ and ⊙ that 'the first is a very slow movement, the next a little faster, and the last a brisk & airry time'. The precise relationship between time signatures broke down during the seventeenth century partly because composers were beginning to use note values too fast to be fitted into the system.

The other reason for the breakdown was uncertainty over the relationship between duple time and triple time. According to the system, three notes in triple time could equal either one in duple time (*tripla*) or two (*sesquialtera*). *Tripla* is the relationship most commonly used by early music groups in seventeenth-century music, for in elaborate, virtuosic music such as Monteverdi's 1610 Vespers the duple-time music demands a crotchet

Ex. 2.4. M. Praetorius, *Polyhymnia caduceatrix et panegyrica* (1619), 'Puer natus in Bethlehem': (a) bb. 31–4; (b) bb. 77–81.

(a)

(b)

rather than a minim beat, which in turn produces unacceptably slow tempos with the *sesquialtera* relationship that the notation theoretically implies. Another option, of course, is the modern relationship in which the length of the bar changes rather than the speed of the notes. There is evidence for this in Michael Praetorius's setting of the Christmas hymn 'Puer natus in Bethlehem' (1619), in which essentially the same music occurs in duple time (Ex. 2.4a) and then in triple time (Ex. 2.4b). It also makes a lot of sense where fast-moving figuration needs to be heard at the same speed in triple time as well as duple time, such as the pavans and galliards in the English virginal repertoire with their elaborate divisions. The modern relationship between duple and triple time seems to have gradually become standard towards the end of the Baroque period, though the frequent changes of time in 'patchwork' seventeenth-century sonatas are best treated proportionally, and the system still works well in larger-scale pieces such as Purcell's *Dido and Aeneas* (1689 or earlier) or J. S. Bach's *Actus tragicus* (Cantata No. 106, *c*.1707), which also have patch-work forms.

Tempo

Tempo became an issue in Western music only when the proportional system broke down, and composers found it necessary to convey their intentions in some other way. One obvious way of doing that was by choosing appropriate note values and time signatures. For instance, the instructions added to Purcell's *A Choice Collection of Lessons* tell us that 3/2 is 'three Minims in a barr, and is commonly play'd very slow', while **3i** has 'three Crotchets in a barr, and they are to be play'd slow'; **3** also has three crotchets a bar but 'is played faster', while 6/4 has 'six Crotchets in a barr & is Commonly to brisk tunes such as Jiggs and Paspys [passepieds]'. In the eighteenth century it became common to use faster note values in 3/8, 6/8, 12/8 and even 24/16, which imply fast tempos, though there must have been some element of 'time signature inflation'; it is likely, for instance, that 6/4 in the seventeenth century was roughly equivalent to 6/8 in the eighteenth. In performing Baroque music you should always consider the possibility that the choice of note values is a clue to the intended tempo.

Another way of defining tempo was to add the Italian words still familiar to us today: adagio, grave, largo, andante, vivace, allegro and presto. Once again Purcell gives us a convenient interpretation, in his *Sonnata's of III Parts* (1683): 'Adagio and Grave, which import nothing but a very slow movement: Presto Largo, Poco Largo, or Largo by it Self, a middle movement: Allegro, and Vivace, a very brisk, Swift, or fast movement'. It is important to realize that at this period the markings described mood as much as tempo: adagio is literally 'at ease', grave 'serious', largo 'large' or 'broad', andante 'walking', allegro and vivace 'lively' or 'cheerful'. The impression that they often just described what was happening in the music is confirmed by the way they frequently accompany changes from slow to fast notes and vice versa, as in Ex. 2.5, from a sonata by Johann Rosenmüller.

The marks gradually acquired the prescriptive force they have today in the course of the eighteenth century, though largo seems to have retained its seventeenth-century meaning as 'a middle movement' throughout the Baroque period: English dictionaries in the 1720s and 30s repeatedly describe it as 'one degree quicker than Grave, and two than Adagio'. In general, there is some anecdotal evidence that tempos were rather faster in the early eighteenth century than in later times, with less difference between slow and fast tempos. In J. S. Bach's obituary (1754), for instance, C. P. E. Bach and Johann Friedrich Agricola wrote: 'In conducting he was very accurate, and of the tempo, which he generally took very lively, he was uncommonly sure'. However, the choice of tempo will depend, as it must have done then, on the type of music, the type of solo instrument or ensemble, the acoustic, the way words are set and, perhaps most import-

antly, the harmonic movement: even experienced performers sometimes forget that a piece with a chord change on every quaver must be played much more slowly than one with only one or two chords a bar.

Ex. 2.5.
J. Rosenmüller,
Sonate (1682):
No. 2 in E minor,
first movement.

Rubato

To what extent should the tempo be varied during the course of a piece? There is no doubt that some types of solo music were played freely. In a famous passage in the preface to his keyboard *Toccate e partite* (1615), Frescobaldi wrote:

> Do not keep strict time throughout but, as in modern [i.e. solo] madrigals, use here a slow tempo, here a fast one, and here one that, as it were, hangs in the air, always in accordance with the expression and meaning of the words.

This sort of freedom was essential to the nature of toccatas, fantasias and free preludes written for solo instruments, even in the eighteenth century, and it presumably should also be applied to the passages of seventeenth-century solo and trio sonatas that use an expressive idiom derived from vocal music. There is also evidence that more conventional ensemble music was sometimes performed in this mannered way – some of John Jenkins's three-part dances written in the 1640s exist in 'humoured' versions with unexpected changes of speed indicated by tempo marks – though in large ensembles the style of performance must have been much more straight-forward, particularly since they were not conducted in the modern sense, and there was often only a minimum of rehearsal. Sending a copy of his ballet *Tirsi e Clori* to the Mantuan court in 1615, Monteverdi suggested that 'if you could let the singers and players see it for an hour before His Highness heard it, it would be a very good thing indeed'.

Dances

Another way of approaching tempo is through dance music, though you should be alert to the possibility that music written for dancing differs from 'abstract' music written in dance forms, such as the dances in eighteenth-century keyboard suites (see also Chapter 3 'Keyboard', pp. 61–3). Also, dances continually changed their character over time, so it is impossible to formulate simple rules that apply to them throughout the time they were popular. In general, dances aged rather as did the people who danced them. For example, the saraband was a wild and licentious dance in its youth in the early seventeenth century, using very simple music with only one or two chords to a bar, demanding to be played one-in-a-bar. In old age, in the 1720s and 30s, it had become a slow and stately dance, often marked 'adagio' or 'lent' and harmonized with six chords to a bar. The exception to this rule is the minuet, which started as a fast one-in-a-bar dance in the mid-seventeenth century, slowed down to a stately three-in-a-bar by Bach and Handel's time, and then speeded up in the second half of the eighteenth century to serve as the model for the scherzo of Beethoven's time. Some eighteenth-century writers tried to fix absolute tempos for dances by refer-ring to the human pulse or pendulums, though the resulting tempos do not always make sense, and it is not clear how accurate the calculations were.

Throughout the Baroque period the French were the leaders of dance fashion: French dancing masters taught the aristocracy of most European countries, and composers all over Europe followed French models when writing their own dance music. A partial exception was Italy, where archaic types of dance music were preserved long after they had disap-peared elsewhere. This is certainly true of the allemande and the courante. The Italian versions, the *allemanda* and *corrente*, preserved the simple rhythms and harmonies of late sixteenth-century dances, and were often marked 'allegro' or 'presto'; they should be played two-in-a-bar and one-in-a-bar respectively. By the late seventeenth century the French allemande was slow, serious and often musically complex, while the courante was usually written in minims and depended for its effect on a graceful alterna-tion between 3/2 and 6/4; J. G. Walther wrote in his *Musicalisches Lexicon* (1732) that it was the 'most solemn' of all dances. Performers today often fail to distinguish between the Italian and French patterns, taking French allemandes and courantes much too fast, and the confusion is compounded by the fact that J. S. Bach, Handel and Corelli included examples of both types in their suites – though Bach often distinguished between *corrente* and *courante* when he labelled them.

Finding the right tempo and character for the other Baroque dances is mostly straightforward, assuming you know when and where the piece was written and are alert to the implications of the notation and harmonic rhythm. The French gavotte normally starts on the half bar, and should be played lightly and elegantly but not too fast, since it usually has at least four chords a bar. By contrast, the Italian *gavotta* often starts on the first beat of the bar, and is sometimes marked 'allegro'. The bourrée and the rigaudon are the fastest duple-time dances of the period: Quantz wrote in his *Versuch einer Anweisung die Flöte traversiere zu spielen* (1752, translated as *On Playing the Flute*) that they should be played 'gaily and with a short and light bow-stroke'. The triple-time hornpipe (not to be confused with the later duple-time type) is usually written in minims, and should be played vigorously but not too fast, since it often has elaborate cross-rhythms and, in Purcell's hands, complex part-writing. The loure is sometimes labelled *pesamment* (heavily), and is a sort of rustic version of the courante. It should be played slowly but extremely strongly, with a marked accent on the first beat of the bar. Like the saraband, the chaconne and passacaglia were wild and fast in the early seventeenth century and slow and stately a century later. The chaconne was usually in the major and more lively than the minor-mode passacaglia, though there are many exceptions and confusions – Purcell's famous Chacony in G minor Z. 730 (*c.*1678) is really a passacaglia – and it is best to be guided by the character of individual pieces.

Minuets come in all shapes and sizes, though they should always be elegant. The earlier type, with essentially one chord a bar, should clearly be played much faster than the three-in-a-bar type. Quantz wrote that the latter 'is played springily, the crotchets being marked with a rather heavy, but still short, bow-stroke'. The passepied is usually in 3/8 rather than 3/4, and is played, according to Quantz, 'a little more lightly and slightly faster' than the minuet. Jigs also come in all shapes and sizes, so it is impossible to generalize about them, though the older types in 6/4 or 6/8 with predominantly dotted rhythms (sometimes called *canaries*) must have been played more slowly than the *moto perpetuo* ones in 12/8 or even 24/16. Dance music can also help us to perform the much larger body of music based to some extent on dance patterns and rhythms. For instance, Purcell's 'Fairest Isle' from *King Arthur* (1691) is a minuet of the late seventeenth-century type, with essentially one chord a bar, and should be sung accordingly, in a gentle one-in-a-bar; 'I know that my Redeemer liveth' from *Messiah* has the character of the later type of minuet, and should be performed larghetto, as Handel marked it, rather than adagio.

Repeats

Mention needs to be made of the problems caused by repeats. The sections of Baroque dance music should normally be repeated, even if repeats are not indicated in the modern way. It was quite common, particularly in the seventeenth century, just to mark off sections with a plain double bar, and in French music repeats were often indicated by a system of signs. There is no reason why you should not add extra repeats to a short dance: patterns sometimes found in the English sets of written-out lute and keyboard variations around 1600 are AABBAB or AABBAABB. Symmetry was important to the Baroque mind. Marc-Antoine Charpentier sometimes specifies that the French *rondeau* should be played AABACAA, and it is likely that Baroque minuets with trios should be played AABBCCDDAABB rather than AABBCCDDAB. The foreshortened pattern seems to have become popular in the late eighteenth century, at a time when it was becoming common not to repeat the second sections of the first movements of symphonies.

Similarly, it seems to have been standard practice to repeat both sections of French overtures, even when the fugue is exceptionally long, as in the overtures to J. S. Bach's orchestral suites. Several early sources of *Messiah* indicate a repeat of the second section of the overture (not marked in most modern editions). You should consider the possibility that sections are meant to be repeated even when the repeats are not specifically indicated, as in the first section of Purcell's *Dido and Aeneas* overture.

Shaping the music

You should not expect to find all the finer aspects of interpretation specified in Baroque music. This is not because it was played without expression, but because composers still mostly left it up to the performer to decide whether a note should be loud or soft, short or long, accented or unaccented; as Quantz put it, 'the good effect of a piece of music depends almost as much upon the performer as upon the composer himself'. Quantz, like many other seventeenth- and eighteenth-century writers, likened music to formal speech:

> Musical execution may be compared with the delivery of an orator. The orator and the musician have, at bottom, the same aim in regard to both the preparation and the final execution of their productions, namely to make themselves masters of the hearts of their listeners, to arouse or still their passions, and to transport them now to this sentiment, now to that.

What this means in practice is that you should aim for a style of interpretation that emphasizes and dramatizes the inherent shapes of the music according to a musical version of the rules of classical rhetoric. Any educated person at the time would have been taught the rules of rhetoric as they applied to literary composition and public speaking, and writers such as Joachim Burmeister (1599, 1601 and 1606), Athanasius Kircher (1650) and Johann Mattheson (1739) showed in detail how they could be applied to music. Musical rhetoric has particular relevance for the treatment of dynamics. By and large, dynamics as we understand them in later music were not important in the Baroque period. An enormous amount of music of all types has no specific dynamics and was just presumed to be *forte*, while the volume of the two main types of keyboard instrument, the organ and the harpsichord, could normally be modified only by changing stops or moving to another manual. Thus you should avoid arbitrary changes of dynamics, particularly when applied to whole sections irrespective of the character of the music, as with the traditional hushed *pianissimo* on the return to the opening of Handel's *Messiah* overture.

It is better to think of dynamics as a resource to be used mainly on the scale of the single phrase. Rising or falling passages often require an increase or decrease of volume, just as an orator should 'raise his voice in words requiring emphasis, subdue it in others', according to Quantz. Long notes usually require a gentle crescendo and decrescendo: the *messa di voce* associated with eighteenth-century Italian singers – not to be confused with the ugly bulges on every note that are still considered good practice by some early music performers. Repeated phrases also usually require added emphasis, though in some contexts repetition can imply an echo – in which case the *piano* is usually indicated in the music.

Most importantly, you should use dynamics to bring out the features of the harmony. Dissonances need to be strong, their resolutions weak. In particular, it is usually best to emphasize the subdominant and dominant chords in cadences, where the dissonances occur, dropping down softly and lightly on to the final tonic chord. The English Restoration writer Roger North wrote in one of his notebooks that 'binding notes' or 'emphaticall discords' should be 'prest hard', adding that 'when you come off into a sweeter calmer air, as to a cadence, which often follows such passages, then be soft and easy, as much to say, Be content all is well'. Quantz ranked dissonances according to whether their strength merited them being played *mezzo-forte*, *forte* or *fortissimo*, and printed a movement for flute and continuo in which the stresses required by the dissonances and their resolutions are exactly specified:

Ex. 2.6. J. J. Quantz, *Versuch einer Anweisung die Flöte traversiere zu spielen* (1752): Affettuoso in E flat, bb. 1–20.

A good way of approaching the process of shaping a piece is to use the harmony to tell you which beats are strong and which are weak. If you are a singer or an accompanist, you will find that strong beats nearly always coincide with the natural stresses of the words, particularly in seventeenth-century music, which tends to be more declamatory and less dominated by abstract musical patterns than eighteenth-century music. For this reason you need to develop an ability to analyse harmony, and that is best done by reading treatises on figured bass (basso continuo); in the Baroque period a knowledge of figured bass was not confined to keyboard players or lutenists, since it was used for teaching harmony as well as for accompanying.

Another basic type of choice you have as a performer is to decide whether to play or sing a note short or long. In the course of the eighteenth century it became common practice to specify the various types of staccato by means of dots, wedges or strokes. Many composers, particularly in England, used wedges as their only type of staccato symbol, presumably to mean all ways of shortening notes, though when the dot was used as well as the wedge or stroke the latter seems to have meant a shorter and more marked note (Ex. 2.7). In the nineteenth century it became common to write such shortenings precisely into the music, increasing the complexity of the notation. But for much of the Baroque period such decisions were still left to the performer.

It is important to realize that the written duration of a note is normally its *maximum* length in performance, and that you can achieve various things by shortening it. What is normally called 'articulation' involves shortening the last note of a phrase or section in order to distinguish it clearly from what follows. In the early seventeenth century the ends of sections were often marked by fermatas (⌢), which sometimes get interpreted as pauses by the unwary today. Articulations of this sort could also be indicated by unexpected breaks in the beams connecting the stems of the notes, or by small oblique dashes, as in Purcell's *Sonnata's of III Parts*. In his *Troisiéme livre de piéces de clavecin* (1722), François Couperin used a comma for this purpose, appropriately likening its effect to punctuation in speech:

> You will find a new sign of which the form is '; this is to mark the ends of melodies or of our harmonic periods, and to make it understood that it is necessary to separate the end of a melody before passing on to that which follows. That is almost imperceptible as a rule, though people of good taste will feel something lacking in the performance if this little silence is not observed; in a word, it is the difference between those who read aloud continuously and those who stop for full-stops and commas; these silences should make themselves felt without altering the time.

Articulation can also be used to emphasize the importance of the note that follows. This is one of the few expressive devices available to the harpsichordist or organist, though it can also be used with profit by players of instruments that can play loud and soft, particularly to achieve strong accents in dance music.

The most basic type of articulation was used to distinguish melodic

material moving by leap from that moving by step. This was apparently so obvious to musicians in the Baroque period, and was so bound up with 'rhetorical' methods of bringing out the inherent shapes in the music, that it was rarely discussed at the time – though a number of writers say that fast movements should be played more articulated than slow movements, which is too much of a generalization to be of use. However, in his discussion of tonguing on the flute, Quantz specified the syllable *ti* 'if you wish to make the notes very short' and *di* 'for slow and sustained notes'; in his example, *ti* is allocated to notes moving by leap and *di* to those moving by step (Ex. 2.8). In fast passage-work, articulation should be used to emphasize leaps,

Ex. 2.7. G. F. Handel, Concerto grosso in F major Op. 6 No. 2, 1739: fourth movement, Allegro ma non troppo, bb. 54–69.

Ex. 2.8. J. J. Quantz, from *Versuch einer Anweisung die Flöte traversiere zu spielen*.

so that the inherent shapes are heard rather than the mechanical accents on the first note of each group.

Baroque composers rarely indicated the basic contrast between detached and sustained playing that is implied by notes moving by leap and by step, though they began to specify slurs in the late seventeenth century. Long lines connecting notes are sometimes found earlier, though usually in a context that suggests that they served as a guide to phrasing rather than an instruction to play legato, or specifically on stringed instruments to take the notes in a single bow. Apart from virtuoso string music, in which elaborate bowings are often specified, slurs are mostly placed in Baroque music over two or three notes, with the intention that they are to be played in a single bow on stringed instruments, with a tonguing that produces a sustained effect on wind instruments, or just legato on other instruments. You should be wary of editions that contain a lot of slurs and apply them across beats or to groups of more than two or three notes: these are likely to have been added by later editors. The classic situation where composers added slurs, and where you should consider doing so if they are missing, is in expressive passages where a pair or pairs of notes fall by step, often resolving a dissonance and sometimes similar in effect to downward-resolving appoggiaturas (Ex. 2.9). Slurs of this sort should always be sung or played, as appoggiaturas should, with the first of the two notes stressed and therefore a little dwelt upon, and the second weak and a little shortened.

Ex. 2.9. J. S. Bach, *Das Orgel-Büchlein*, mostly 1713–15: *O Lamm Gottes unschuldig* BWV 618, bb. 1–2.

National styles

There was little difference between the idioms used by Renaissance composers in all European countries, and apparently little variation in the ways musicians in different countries performed their music. However, important differences developed during the seventeenth century between Italian and French music, and by 1700 their distinct dialects looked as if they might turn into mutually unintelligible languages. Handel's first biographer John Mainwaring (1760) told a story about Corelli and the first sections of Handel's French overtures which may or may not be true but certainly illustrates the point:

Several fruitless attempts HANDEL had one day made to instruct him [Corelli] in the manner of executing these spirited passages. Piqued at the tameness with which he still played them, he [Handel] snatches the instrument out of his hand; and, to convince him how little he understood them, played the passages himself. But CORELLI, who was a person of great modesty and meekness, wanted no conviction of this sort; for he declared that he did not understand them; i.e. knew not how to execute them properly, and give them the strength and expression they required. When HANDEL appeared impatient, *Ma, caro Sassone* (said he) *questa Musica è nel stylo Francese di ch'io non m'intendo* [But dear Saxon, this music is in the French style which I don't understand].

In François Couperin's programmatic trios, *Le Parnasse, ou L'apothéose de Corelli* (1724) and *Concert instrumental sous le titre d'Apothéose composé à la mémoire immortelle de l'incomparable Monsieur de Lully* (1725), the different styles of Italian and French music were associated with the composers who came to define them around 1700. The latter concludes with a trio sonata (or 'Sonade en trio', as Couperin called it) that demonstrates how 'the union of the French and Italian styles must create musical perfection'. Much orchestral and chamber music by Handel, J. S. Bach, Telemann and their contemporaries is concerned with the same issue, and requires the performer to distinguish between the French and Italian elements.

The differences between the styles arose partly because French music was much more conservative than Italian music, and preserved features of Renaissance musical practice into the eighteenth century. The French retained the archaic five-part type of orchestral writing, with a single violin part and three viola parts; they continued to use the viol as a solo instrument; they continued to use older types of vocal writing, with a fluid relationship between *récit* and *air*; and they were reluctant to use 'abstract' Italian musical forms such as the concerto and the sonata – most French Baroque music of all types is based in some way on dance music. In general, French music stood for delicacy, decorum, elegant melody and graceful *agréments*, while Italian music stood for passion, extravagance, virtuosity and florid ornamentation or *passaggi*. Too often performers today fail to respect these differences, performing Italian music with inappropriate restraint and French music without its refined performing conventions.

Altering rhythms

The basic difference between the performance of French and Italian music was that French musicians altered notated rhythms in performance to a greater extent than Italian musicians. François Couperin wrote in *L'art de toucher le clavecin* (1716):

> We write [music] differently from the way we play it, which causes foreigners to play our music less well than we play theirs. By contrast the Italians write their music in the true note values in which they intended them [to be performed]. For example, we dot groups of quavers moving by step despite the fact that we write them equal. Our custom has enslaved us, and we continue with it.

This effect, commonly called *notes inégales* (unequal notes), was not confined to France or French-style music around 1700, and was described by writers such as Loys Bourgeois (1550), Tomás de Santa María (1565), Giovanni Battista Bovicelli (1594), Giulio Romolo Caccini (1602) and Frescobaldi (1615). The consensus was that groups of apparently equal fast notes in written-out *passaggi* or divisions could be performed unevenly, either long–short or short–long. It was also applied to seventeenth-century dance music, as is suggested by the variants between different versions of the same piece. In the following example, a masque dance by Robert Johnson (*c.*1583–1633), the plain version (Ex. 2.10a) comes from an ensemble setting used by professional wind players, while the dotted keyboard setting (Ex. 2.10b) was probably intended for amateurs; music written out for amateurs tended to be more accurately notated than that used by professionals, who would have been familiar with the rules of elegant performance. The author of the *Burwell Lute Tutor* (*c.*1670) wrote about 'the Soule of the lute', which consisted of 'stealing halfe a note from one note and bestoweing of it upon the next note' to 'make the playing of the Lute more Aerye and skipping'. He added that 'The heareing of Violins and singing is a great helpe to learne this livelines and Sweetnes'. Inequality was probably widely used all over Europe at the time to make dance music more elegant, as jazz is 'swung' today.

Ex. 2.10.
R. Johnson, Almand,
*c.*1615, bb. 1–8:
(a) ensemble setting
melody line;
(b) keyboard setting.

 Notes inégales seem to have been used in virtually all types of French Baroque music, and it is possible to formulate reasonably precise rules for them from writers around 1700 such as Jean Rousseau (1687), Étienne Loulié (1696) and Monsieur de Saint Lambert (1702). Inequality should be gentle rather than aggressive, achieved by playing pairs of notes strong–weak rather than by markedly changing even notes to dotted notes, and it should be applied to the fastest predominant note values so long as the tempo allows; it is impracticable to play very fast notes unequally. It should not be applied to groups of repeated notes, or to notes that move by leap rather than step; and composers developed ways of indicating when they wanted equal notes, by placing dots over them, or by using terms such as *détaché*, *notes égales* or *marqué*. You should also consider applying *notes inégales* to music in the French style written outside France, though it was more common in other countries to write out music with dotted notes, in which case rhythms such as those in Ex. 2.11 may have to be played *less* dotted than written. However, when written dotted rhythms are juxtaposed

with apparently even notes in the same piece, as in Ex. 2.12, it usually works best if they are sharply contrasted.

Another type of rhythmic alteration involved changing the length of notes to fit into a prevailing rhythm. It was not confined to French or French-style music, and was used by composers as a type of shorthand to

Ex. 2.11. H. Purcell, *A Choice Collection of Lessons for the Harpsichord or Spinnet* (1696): Suite No. 7 in D minor Z. 668, Almand 'Bell-barr', bb. 1–9.

Ex. 2.12. (below) H. Purcell, *King Arthur* (1691): Chaconne, bb. 37–48.

avoid notating complex rhythms precisely, particularly before the double dot became popular in the middle of the eighteenth century. It usually involved playing notes later than written to fit into prevailing dotted patterns, as in Ex. 2.13; though it could involve playing notes earlier than written, so that they coincide with triplets, as in the Italianate Corrente of Bach's keyboard Partita No. 1 in B flat major BWV 825, or the Tempo di Gavotta quoted in Ex. 2.14. That said, there are cases in Baroque music where the differing characters of music in triplets and duple time suggest that they should not be reconciled, such as the triplet horn calls in the first movement of Bach's Brandenburg Concerto No. 1, or the Giga by Corelli quoted in Ex. 2.15. ①

Ex. 2.13. H. Purcell, *Sonnata's of III Parts* (1683): No. 7 in E minor, bb. 80–91, Largo (bb. 9–20).

Ex. 2.14. J. S. Bach, Six Partitas (1731): No. 6 in E minor BWV 830, Tempo di Gavotta, bb. 1–5.

Ex. 2.15. A. Corelli,
Sonate da camera a tre
Op. 2 (1685): No. 9 in
F sharp minor, third
movement, Giga,
bb. 1–4.

You should certainly be wary of altering the rhythms of vocal music, for doing so can easily obscure the words or throw stresses on to the wrong words. For instance, there is no justification for changing Purcell's carefully calculated rhythms in the recitatives of *Dido and Aeneas*, as the Novello vocal score does, or shortening the 'The' in 'The Lord gave the word' from *Messiah*. Johann Mattheson wrote in 1737 that 'If the French, whom I regard as great masters in instrumental style, had to forgo the dots beside the notes, they would be like cooks without salt'. But he added: 'For it is certain that such sharpened rhythms, so beautiful and cheerful for instruments, make no such agreeable effect in the throat of a singer, and are to be regarded, so to say, as foreigners in vocal melody (and only such) when they occasionally appear'.

French overtures

All the problems surrounding rhythmic alteration in Baroque music come together in the first sections of French overtures. Until recently it was accepted that, in the words of Thurston Dart, 'all the parts should move together, jerkily, even when their written note-values do not suggest that this is how they should be played. *All* dotted rhythms should be adjusted so that they fit the shortest one in the piece'. Dart's example, the opening of the overture to Lully's *Alceste* (1674), makes his point graphically (Ex. 2.16). The existence of this over-dotted or double-dotted style has been called into question in recent years by Frederick Neumann and others, and there has been a partial return to performing overtures more or less as written. In fact, as Stephen Hefling points out in his thorough investigation of the subject (1993), no single approach works with the whole repertoire. Some pieces, such as the overtures to Charpentier's opera *Actéon* (1683–5), Purcell's *Amphitryon* suite (1690) or Bach's Suite No. 1 in C major for orchestra (*c*.1723), open with sections that are similar to allemandes, and only really work played more or less as written, with *notes inégales* where necessary.

Equally, there is hard evidence for over-dotting in Quantz, and in such things as the two versions of Bach's keyboard Overture 'in the French Style' (1735), or the alterations the organist and composer Jonathan Battishill made around 1785 to a printed keyboard transcription of Handel's *Partenope* overture (Ex. 2.17). Of course, the effect of both approaches depends crucially on the speed adopted: the slower the tempo, the more important it is to decide exactly where the dotted notes are going

Ex. 2.16. J. B. Lully, *Alceste* (1674): overture, bb. 1–4 (a) as written; (b) as interpreted by Thurston Dart.

to be placed. What evidence there is suggests that the first sections of seventeenth-century overtures were performed in two rather than four – $\text{半} = 64$ is recorded for the overture of Pascal Collasse's opera *Thétis et Pélée* (1689) – and it may be that the practice of over-dotting developed as a way of maintaining the essentially lively character of the overture as its speed declined in the eighteenth century.

Ex. 2.17. G. F. Handel, *Partenope* (1730): overture, bb. 1–8 (a) as published by M. Wright (*c.*1785); (b) altered by Jonathan Battishill.

Ornaments

As already mentioned, there are two main types of ornaments: *passaggi* or divisions and *agréments* or graces. They are associated with Italian and French music respectively, though a basic repertoire of graces was used all over Europe. Graces decorate a single note rather than a group of notes, and consist of two main types, trills and appoggiaturas; turns became important only in mid-eighteenth-century music, while mordents were largely confined to lute and keyboard music. French late seventeenth- and early eighteenth-century composers usually took care to indicate *agréments* accurately, and often provided tables which show how they are to be interpreted; a good example is the one printed by Couperin in his *Pieces de clavecin...premier livre* (Ex. 2.18). Thus you will encounter most problems with earlier seventeenth-century music and the music of other countries. English virginal music, for instance, uses two main ornament signs: a single oblique stroke or a pair of strokes drawn through the stems of notes, or above, below or through semibreves and breves. However, no contemporary source explains them, no single interpretation works in all situations, and the placing of the signs tends to vary in different sources of particular pieces; the impression given is that English keyboard composers liked their music ornamented, but did not care too much exactly how it was done.

It is often assumed that trills in the Baroque period should always start on the upper note, but this is far from the case. The keyboard *tremoli* and *tremoletti* discussed by Girolamo Diruta (1593) begin on the note, while Caccini's sung *gruppo* is an extended accelerating trill starting on the leading note of a cadence; his *trillo* also accelerates, but consists of reiterations of a single note (Ex. 2.19). A table by Charles Coleman (Ex. 2.20) illustrates various types of trills or 'shaked graces' starting on the note and above the note, to be played 'with one motion of the Bow'. Late seventeenth-century sources, such as the 'Rules for Graces' added to Purcell's *A Choice Collection of Lessons*, suggest that by then trills usually started from the upper note with an appoggiatura or *tremblement appuyé*; though even in late Baroque music you should consider starting trills on the note in certain circumstances, such as when the appoggiatura removes a dissonance or when you need to develop a trill in the middle of a long note. In general, trills should be graceful rather than aggressive, and you may need to add a termination or an anticipation of the cadence note even if it is not specified. Trills are usually indicated by the signs *t.*, *tr*, ⬝⬝⬝, + or ⫽, though many composers did not bother to indicate them; you should always add them to standard cadence formulas, and you should consider adding them in most cadential situations, particularly where the melodic line rises 7–1 or falls 2–1.

Appoggiaturas are particularly associated with late Baroque music, though they undoubtedly existed earlier. For instance, the manuscripts of early seventeenth-century English songs sometimes include / and \ signs in front of notes, apparently indicating upward and downward slides, and Coleman's ornament table includes both types among the 'smooth graces', described respectively as a 'beat' and a 'backfall'; the latter is indicated by a comma. In the late seventeenth century the appoggiatura became one of

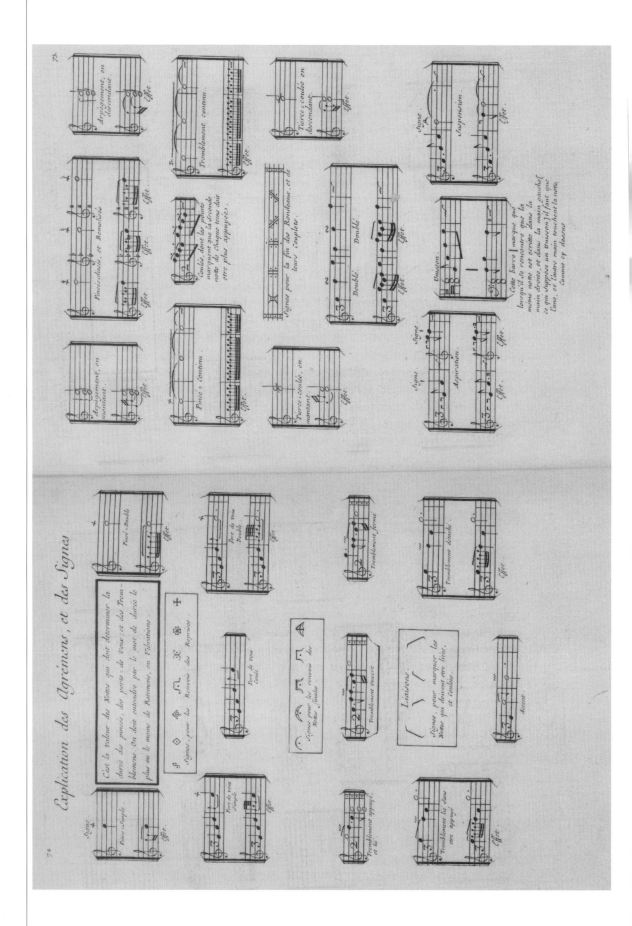

Ex. 2.18. (opposite)
F. Couperin, *Pieces de
clavecin...premier livre*
(1713): pp. 74–5.
(See also Ex. 3.1,
p. 52.)

Ex. 2.19.
G. R. Caccini, *Le
nuove musiche* (1602):
examples of trills.

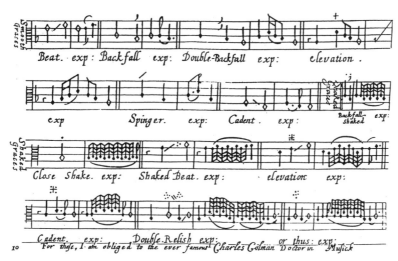

Ex. 2.20. C. Coleman,
table of ornaments
from C. Simpson, *The
Division-Violist*
(1659).

the principal ornaments in French or French-style music, as can be seen in
the example illustrating ornaments in John Lenton's violin treatise *The
Gentleman's Diversion* (Ex. 2.21); Lenton was a long-standing colleague of
Henry Purcell in the English court orchestra, the Twenty-Four Violins. You
should normally play appoggiaturas on the beat, except when they act as
tierces coulés, filling in the gap between falling 3rds, when you should play
them lightly just in front of the beat. Seventeenth-century appoggiaturas
seem to have been played quite short – Purcell gives the 'forefall' and the
'backfall' in his 'Rules for Graces' as semiquaver, dotted-quaver patterns –
though things had changed by the mid-eighteenth century. J. S. Bach and
his contemporaries frequently wrote them with long note-values, and the

Ex. 2.21. J. Lenton,
*The Gentleman's
Diversion* (1693):
examples of
ornaments.

examples in Quantz suggest they should be as long as possible, taking half of ordinary notes, two-thirds of dotted notes, the whole of the first of two tied notes in compound time, and even the whole note when it is followed by a rest, pushing the resolution into the silence.

Vibrato

Contrary to popular belief, vibrato was used in the Baroque period. Writers mention the 'close shake', *tremolo*, *flattement* or *Bebung* as a type of ornament used to imitate the natural vibration of sound. Leopold Mozart wrote in his treatise on violin playing (1756) that it is 'an ornamentation which arrives from Nature herself and which can be used charmingly on a long note, not only by good instrumentalists but also by clever singers'. He went on to compare it to the 'trembling after sound' heard when a slack string or a bell is struck sharply, while Roger North described it as

> a gentle and slow wavering, not into a trill, upon the swelling [of] the note; such as trumpetts use, as if the instrument were a little shaken with the wind of its owne sound, but not so as to vary the tone [pitch], which must be religiously held to its place, like a pillar on its base, without the least loss of the accord.

Thus, vibrato should not alter the pitch and affect the tuning. It was used on long notes, often associated with the *messa di voce*, and it should be particularly avoided in fast passage-work, since it affects the clarity of part-writing. Continuous vibrato was not generally used in orchestras until the twentieth century.

Florid ornamentation

An important part of the training of professional musicians in the sixteenth century was the technique of improvising florid ornamentation – called at the time *passaggi* or divisions. The technique was explained in a number of Italian treatises published from the 1580s to the 1620s, and the examples included in them are useful models to help you apply your own ornamentation to the music of the period. In the seventeenth century, *passaggi* were increasingly incorporated by composers into the fabric of the music, though florid ornamentation was applied to the slow movements of Italian sonatas and concertos throughout the Baroque period, and Italian singers were expected to improvise it in the repeated sections of opera arias throughout the eighteenth century. Ornamentation was particularly expected at the 6/4 chords before the final cadences of the vocal sections of opera arias, and the equivalent places in concertos (later formalized in the Classical period as the cadenza), or the series of cadential chords that often link movements in concerti grossi. The written-out examples of cadenzas that survive suggest that they should be brief; Quantz recommended that cadenzas in flute concertos should take only a single breath. There is no historical justification for the common practice of adding a complete composed movement to the two chords that punctuate Bach's Brandenburg Concerto No. 3, or for allowing continuo players to decorate cadences; it was taken for granted that that was the privilege of the soloist or the leader of the ensemble.

The best-known examples of florid ornamentation are the ornamented versions of some of the slow movements of Corelli's Op. 5 violin sonatas, published by Roger of Amsterdam in 1710 with the claim that they were 'composed by Corelli as he plays them' (Ex. 2.22). They are similar to written-out ornamentation in the slow movements of sonatas, published in London, by J. C. Pepusch (*c.*1707), William Babell (*c.*1725) and others. The basic technique involved connecting up the notes of the melody with runs moving largely by step, though surviving written-out examples suggest that by the middle of the eighteenth century a more varied style had developed, with graces and broken chords as well as runs.

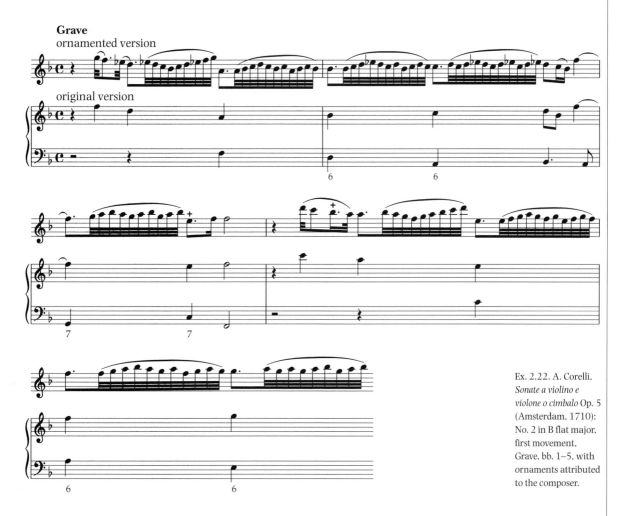

Ex. 2.22. A. Corelli, *Sonate a violino e violone o cimbalo* Op. 5 (Amsterdam, 1710): No. 2 in B flat major, first movement, Grave, bb. 1–5, with ornaments attributed to the composer.

You should be careful not to apply florid ornamentation to the wrong type of music. It seems to have been avoided in French or French-style music, and its use is questionable in English Restoration music. In the preface to his *Little Consort* (1656), Matthew Locke asked performers to 'do yourselves and me the right to play plain, not Tearing them in pieces with division', while even in the early eighteenth century Roger North thought the Corelli ornaments printed by Roger 'so much vermin'.

Conclusion

I have emphasized the fact that 'Baroque music' is not a single phenom-enon, to be performed in only one way. You should always be acutely aware of when, where and why the music you are performing was written, and to what genre it belongs. But all music of the period will benefit from a style of performance that projects its essential characteristics as sharply and vividly as possible.

Davitt Moroney

17

Keyboard

Introduction

Keyboard instruments during the seventeenth and eighteenth centuries were similar to those used throughout the Renaissance, but presented some significant developments. They may be divided into three main categories: organs (which are wind instruments; Baroque organs are always operated by a purely mechanical tracker action directly linking the keyboard to the pipes); harpsichords (including spinets and virginals, all of which use plucked strings); and clavichords (which have gently hammered strings). Although early pianos were coming into use by the middle of the eighteenth century, their impact on styles of performance was felt only at the end of the century and they are not discussed here.

Understanding how Baroque music may have been played on all these early instruments is stimulating and instructive for the increasingly large number of players who respond to their uniquely expressive qualities. It can also help those who play the same music on modern pianos or organs, by identifying the kinds of musical expression the composer would probably have known and perhaps expected. It is useful to think about what aspects of performance were considered significant in the Baroque period and to try and make these same features contribute to modern piano performances, without denying the nature of the piano itself, or trying to imitate the older instruments. The parts of this chapter apparently written for harpsichordists and organists are thus also addressed to pianists.

Although the organ, harpsichord and clavichord are very different instruments, nobody during the Renaissance and Baroque periods would have thought it normal to separate the players into different categories, according to which instrument they played. Many of the greatest harpsichordists of the period (J. S. Bach, François Couperin, Jean-Philippe Rameau, for example) earned their living mainly as organists at certain periods of their life. Much repertoire is shared by all the instruments, although certain pieces may be played differently depending on which instrument is used (faster speed, more elaborate style of ornamentation, more extreme articulation). Harpsichordists who play the organ music of Bach and Couperin, for example, will recognize more easily the various styles they use. Similarly, organists who know Bach's *Das wohltemperirte Clavier* (The Well-Tempered Clavier) or Couperin's *L'art de toucher le clavecin* will have little difficulty developing the delicate touch needed on tracker-action organs. And pianists who understand both harpsichord and organ can develop more varied ways of playing their own instrument.

Keyboard technique, fingering and ornaments

Baroque keyboard teachers seem to have been relatively unconcerned about precise fingering and to have spent more time teaching correct hand position. Good fingering is largely the result of good hand position, not the other way round. Baroque keyboard technique, even at its most developed (as for Bach's Goldberg Variations, for example), requires the hands and fingers to be kept at all times in a compact but relaxed form, described by one sixteenth-century writer as being like a cat's paw. They should be moved around the keyboard without being altered by too many extensions and contractions. The movement of the hands should be strictly from left to right or right to left, in a line that is parallel to the keyboard. It should, if possible, be a small and precise movement from the wrist or (but only if necessary) from the elbow. It should never be a movement at right angles to this left–right axis (i.e. a movement parallel to the individual keys) since such a movement disturbs the whole arm from the shoulders down.

Fig. 3.1. South German eighteenth-century picture of a clavichord player, showing good hand position.

The German composer Friedrich Wilhelm Marpurg summarized important attitudes to hand position that were shared by the best players all over Europe for nearly two centuries. He wrote:

> the position of the fingers is not such an arbitrary thing as many players think. It is true that there are passages that can be fingered in more than one way. But of all these ways, there is always one which is more suitable to these passages than any other... One should therefore choose among the good positions... And then, between these different possible positions, one must choose the one that makes the least movement. (*Principes du clavecin*, 1756, first published as *Die Kunst das Clavier zu spielen*, 1750.)

Movement of the body or arms while playing was not considered, as is sometimes the case today, to be a sign of musicality, or of expressive playing. On the contrary, the principle of limiting movement as much as possible was considered important in all countries. (Couperin, in addition, suggests putting a small mirror on the music desk in front of players who make grimaces!) Body movement was universally condemned as damaging to a good keyboard technique. Bach can serve as an absolutely reliable model here:

> [He] played with a fingering that was so easy and relaxed it was almost invisible. Only the outer joints of the fingers moved. His hand maintained its curved shape, even in the most difficult passages. The fingers almost never left the keys... The other parts of his body...did not move at all.
> (J. N. Forkel, *Ueber Johann Sebastian Bachs Leben, Kunst und Kunstwerke*, 1802, based partly on correspondence with Bach's sons.)

Rameau's short but brilliant *De la mechanique des doigts sur le clavessin* (1724) is the most precious of all Baroque texts about keyboard technique. He comments 'I will put down the rules and I think that one can hardly be allowed not to follow them exactly, step by step, since they are based on reason'. The most important ideas are as follows:

- The elbows should always 'fall nonchalantly' to the side of the body, in a relaxed and natural position.
- Fingers 1 and 5 of each hand should always remain 'on the keyboard', in contact with the keys 'as if stuck to them', and fingers 2, 3 and 4 should be curved in such a way as to remain at all times in front of the sharps, not between them. (Letting the hands fall in a relaxed way to the side of the body shows the degree of curve needed, although players with long fingers may need to curve 2 and 3 just a little more when they lift the hands back on to the keyboard.)
- The movement of the fingers starts 'at the point where the finger is rooted in the hand and never anywhere else; the movement of the hand is at the wrist. Should it ever be necessary to move the arm, this is done from the elbow'. Rameau excludes all movement from the shoulders in the course of normal playing (it is only required for hand crossing). When one finger plays a note, 'no other fingers should move'.
- 'A greater movement should only ever take place when a smaller one is not sufficient; and so when a finger can reach a key without moving the hand, merely by extending and opening it [the finger], one must be careful not to move more than is necessary'.
- Above all, the hands 'must at all times support the fingers; the fingers must never support the hands... Never add weight to the touch of the fingers by an effort of the hand; on the contrary, let your hand, by supporting the fingers, make their touch more light. This is of great consequence'. This last point is perhaps the single most important principle. If your wrist rises when you play a note or a chord, then the fingers are (wrongly) supporting the hand.

The familiar notion that the thumb was not used in Baroque keyboard music until Bach is a great oversimplification. The thumb has always been considered necessary at the start of right-hand scales, or the end of left-hand ones, and it was normal to use it on notes adjacent to accidentals, as well as in three-note chords or chordal patterns. Its use was certainly somewhat more restricted than in the nineteenth century, and it was avoided as much as possible on sharps and flats. Only fingers 2, 3 and 4 were generally placed on the accidentals, except in cases of absolute necessity such as octaves on sharps or flats (requiring both 1 and 5 together). 5 was used even more rarely than 1, mostly in three-note chords or chordal patterns and in the context of large intervals such as octaves, which occur more frequently in the left hand. Longer fingers were allowed to pass over shorter ones: 3 over 4 or 2; 4 over 5; and 2 over 1. They can do this as easily as the shorter ones can be passed under 3. Harpsichordists and organists will find such fingerings not only historical but helpful. Pianists may also be surprised by the extent to which they are suitable for Baroque music.

Baroque ornaments in the right hand are usually played with the fingers 2 and 3 or 3 and 4. Those in the left hand mostly use 1 and 2 or 2 and 3. Simple ornaments (trills, mordents, turns, arpeggios) almost always begin precisely on the beat. Nevertheless, Jean Henry d'Anglebert (1689, see Ex. 3.1) and Couperin (1713, see Ex. 2.18, p. 44) both codified various complex ornaments that start before the beat and some particularly subtle ones that start after the beat. Since Bach's keyboard ornamentation is derived from that of the best French musicians, and from d'Anglebert and Couperin in particular, it is impossible without studying these two great keyboard composers to understand the full range and variety of ornaments Bach expected to be used. In French-style ornamentation (which was also used by, for example, Purcell and Handel), trills usually start on the upper note. Domenico Scarlatti, on the other hand, following Italian practice, may well not have expected all the trills to start on the upper note; a main-note trill often suits his sonatas better.

Rolled or arpeggiated chords start with the bass on the beat (rather than starting before the beat and rolling up to the last note on the beat). Baroque arpeggiation, as shown in the detailed notation of Louis Couperin's

Ex. 3.1.
J. H. d'Anglebert,
Pieces de clavecin
(1689): table of
ornaments.

unmeasured preludes (Ex. 3.2) or Froberger's works, was very varied and by no means restricted to a simple rolling of the chord from bass to treble. Sometimes chords are arpeggiated downwards, especially right-hand chords where the top note is the main melody note. More complex and imaginative chords are also frequently appropriate, with the right hand rolling down rapidly while the left rolls up slowly, for example.

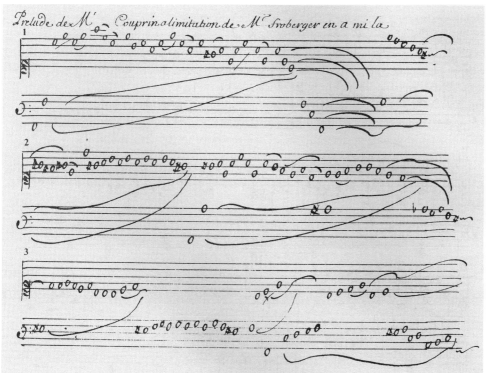

Ex. 3.2. L. Couperin, opening of *Prélude à l'imitation de Monsieur Froberger.* Louis Couperin, uncle of François 'le grand', was one of the main exponents of the unmeasured prelude, in which the rhythms and durations of notes are left to the player.

Baroque instruments, touch and musical discourse

All organs of the Renaissance and Baroque periods (and modern tracker instruments built in similar styles) have a light mechanical action, giving the player an extremely precise control over the nature of the attack at the start of each note, no matter how many stops are used at once. Touch is one of the most significant features that distinguishes Baroque organs from many later instruments. The player can decide exactly how the wind starts to enter the pipe, sharply and cleanly, or gently. If the finger plays or leaves a note more slowly, the sound at the start or end of the note is changed, and softened.

Having access to a tracker-action organ can teach a modern player more about the expressive nature of Baroque touch than any number of lessons on an organ with electronic action. However, sensitivity to varied touch and delicate finger control can make a noticeable difference on any modern organ, even a purely electronic one. Judges of good organ playing pay particular attention to the question.

On the harpsichord, also, the player can control quite significantly the nature of the start of the note, of the attack. This is especially true of instruments with quills – the plectrum part of the mechanism that actually plucks the string – cut from bird feathers (as was done in the Baroque period; the favoured bird was the crow), rather than from the modern plastic which has become an all too easy solution nowadays. Furthermore, the key-dip on harpsichords that are correctly regulated is much less than on a piano, and the plucking point is quite high: the key has to move only about two or three millimetres before the string sounds. This, along with very rapid escapement mechanism (of which the essential element is a spring made of a thick bristle from a boar's back), means less movement is required of the fingers, thus making possible much faster trills, for example. As François Couperin noted in 1716, although the harpsichord cannot play crescendos and diminuendos, it 'nevertheless has its own proper characteristics, which are brilliance, clarity and precision'. These qualities, which are directly derived from the nature of the mechanics of the action, amply compensate for the relative lack of dynamic contrast. The piano certainly gained in dynamic range, but the price to pay was, quite literally, heavy, since the action is heavier and slower.

Fig. 3.2. Single-manual harpsichord made by Pascal Taskin, signed and dated 1786.

Helpful parallels are found in other instruments from the period. Players of the recorder and flute used varied 'tonguing' techniques, namely different ways of using the tongue as if pronouncing a consonant at the start of the sound. Normally this was a 't', to give a good attack. Sixteenth- and early seventeenth-century treatises give a variety of tonguings for groups of semiquavers. Using the 't' tonguing on its own ('tu-tu-tu-tu...') makes the notes more staccato, but it is difficult to do rapidly. In faster passages notes can be made more elegant by being paired ('tu-re, tu-re'), played in groups of fours ('tu-re-lu-re, tu-re-lu-re'), or in eights ('tu-re-lu-re du-re-lu-re, tu-re-lu-re du-re-lu-re').

Good playing of Baroque music on old or modern keyboards depends on a varied touch that is similar to these varied tonguings. Control of variety of attack is essential for making the music expressive. The fingers can be used to vary the attack in ways comparable to the 't' 'd' 'l' and 'r' tonguings (here presented in decreasing order of attack). Differences in quality of the attack are more useful than differences in volume. They can be produced by speed of attack, as they can also on the piano. (Specifically, the difference of touch changes the balance of the upper harmonics.) This gives both harpsichordists and organists a wide range of technical means of controlling and shaping a phrase, by increasing stress and intensity on important notes – that is, expressing the subtle nuances of the composer's musical thought by means of an audible artistic discourse.

Bach's desire to teach his pupils to play in a singing manner ('eine Cantable Art'), expressed on the title page of the fifteen two-part Inventions and fifteen three-part Sinfonias (1723), should not be confused with a search for an exaggeratedly legato style of playing. Varied touch is as essential to musical discourse on all keyboards as consonants are to language. Singers sustain syllables on vowels but use consonants to define the words and meaning of a text. In a comparable way, the sustained notes on all keyboards (especially the organ) are like vowels, and the absolute necessity of developing a variety of touch, that is, of attack at the start of each note, provides the 'consonants' so that the instrumental cantabile can sing with richer musical meaning. On the organ and harpsichord, playing that suffers from the absence of varied attacks is like a rather primitive language that may have five vowels but has only a few consonants. If you remove the consonants from the word 'cantabile', you are left with a meaningless '-a- -a-i-e'; if, on the other hand, you remove the vowels then you have 'c-nt-b-l-', a stunted but recognizable word. An absolutely legato style of playing in effect removes all the consonants from the musical discourse.

Although players are expected to find ways of increasing and decreasing tension and other ways of directing the listeners' ears, notably through the variety of touch that remains the basis of good playing, musical effects using crescendo and diminuendo are not out of place in keyboard music. Their evident presence and appropriateness in works using flutes, violins, viols or voices confirms the extent to which they are a natural part of Baroque music.

Moreover, such gradations of volume are possible on the clavichord, which was considered the ideal learning instrument. Bach no doubt intended players of his Inventions and Sinfonias to develop their 'singing manner' on the clavichord at first. Their keyboard is restricted to the traditional four-octave range of German clavichords at that time (*C–c'''*, the same range as many of Bach's so-called French Suites and the first volume of *Das wohltemperirte Clavier*). Works such as the Chromatic Fantasia and Fugue were probably also often played on the clavichord. Bach's first biographer J. N. Forkel commented that 'the clavichord was his favourite instrument... He considered it to be the best instrument, either for studying or for playing in private. He liked using it to express his finest thoughts'.

Although only a few pieces were specifically composed for the clavichord, almost all keyboard music, including organ music, was played and

Fig. 3.3. Clavichord made by Ugo Annibale Traeri of Modena, 1726. It contains a hand-written label saying 'This clavichord belonged to Handel, who used it in composition, when travelling...'

practised on it, especially at home. It was certainly not limited to delicate little pieces. The composer Johann Mattheson wrote in 1713 (in *Das neu-eröffnete Orchestre*) that as a keyboard instrument the clavichord was 'beloved above all others' and specifically recommended it for playing 'over-tures, sonatas, toccatas, suites, etc.' Composers of the generation after Bach were also much influenced by the instrument, especially the later models with five octaves (F'–f'''). C. P. E. Bach wrote many pieces for it (notably his magnificent *Abschied von meinem Silbermannischen Claviere*, Farewell to my Silbermann Clavichord, 1781). The dynamic indications in his works were intended to help clavichord players, though they can still help pianists, of course. The same may well be true of many of Haydn's early keyboard sonatas. A surviving portrait of Haydn shows him seated at a clavichord.

On the clavichord, the hammer remains in contact with the string for as long as the key is depressed. If the player presses a little harder, pressure is put directly on the string, which rises a little in pitch. In this way careful finger control can produce a vibrato, known by the German word *Bebung* (notated with three dots over the note). The clavichord is the only keyboard instrument before the invention of the electronic ondes martenot in 1928 that uses vibrato as an expressive ornament. (Most Baroque organs have a tremblant stop that can impose a regular mechanical vibrato on all the notes; this can be astonishingly expressive, as long as the player adjusts the speed of the piece so that the rhythm of the short notes relates to the speed of the mechanical vibrato.)

On old organs and harpsichords changes to the registration have to be made manually, during an appropriate rest in at least one hand (harpsi-chord pedals were a twentieth-century invention). They may often be seen more as changes of colour than of volume. Swell boxes (allowing the player to vary the extent to which the pipes are enclosed and so create crescendos and diminuendos) were developed gradually from the late seventeenth century onwards, especially in England, but they were rare and remain largely foreign to the needs of organ music from continental Europe. They have no place in the performance of works by J. S. Bach.

English organs lacked pedals until the later eighteenth century, and many instruments still did not have them in the nineteenth century. 16' tone (sounding an octave below the written note) is therefore not needed on the bass line of early English music and was not expected by the composers. Continental organs used the pedals a good deal, as early as the later fifteenth century in the Germanic tradition. In Germany, the Pedal Organ developed into a completely independent organ, with a wide range of stops capable of supporting the Great without being coupled to it. An over-reliance on the Pedal coupled to the Great is not historical.

As for pedal technique itself, only the toes were generally used, not the heel, especially in faster passages such as semiquavers. This is confirmed by the first part of J. C. H. Rinck's remarkable *Praktische Orgelschule* (1819), where the first fifty-two of the eighty-six pedal exercises use only the toes, and cover the whole range of pedal technique needed to play Bach's music. (The modern technique based on movement from the ankle came into general use in the later nineteenth century.)

Fig. 3.4. The organ of the abbey at Weingarten. Built by Joseph Gabler between 1737 and 1750. Copper engraving, 1770.

Continuo accompaniment

One important function of keyboard instruments has always been to accompany: either partnering a solo singer or instrumentalist or in a larger ensemble. A few well-known eighteenth-century chamber pieces include a fully written-out, or 'obbligato', keyboard part (sonatas by J. S. Bach, C. P. E.

Bach and Boismortier, for example). However, the vast majority of Baroque accompaniments take the form of a 'continuo' or 'figured bass'. (These terms are derived from the Italian *basso continuo* and the French *basse chiffrée*.) Continuo realizations are not always played on keyboards; instruments of the lute family, and even the harp, can be used. Nevertheless, keyboard realizations were the most common practical accompaniments, and remain so today.

A figured bass consists of a bass line with numbers above or below some of the notes, indicating the harmonies that the continuo player is expected to fill in, at the very least on the main beats. Jazz pianists and rhythm guitarists in contemporary popular music have much in common with continuo players since they also read from chord symbols, although the system they use is somewhat different. Since the harmonies are played above the bass line, Baroque scores more frequently position the numbers above the bass. (Modern practice usually places them below, although this is less logical.)

The system used for figuring the bass is very simple. For example, a '3' indicates that the player must add the note which is the interval of a diatonic 3rd above the bass note, whereas a '6' indicates the addition of the 6th. If these notes are not diatonic and require chromatic alteration because of a modulation, the figures can carry additional sharps or flats (sometimes placed before the figure, sometimes after); or the figure may be crossed through. But in practice the notation is a little cryptic. Two examples will make this clear:

- What is not indicated is often more important than what is. The absence of any figuring at all usually implies the figures '5' and '3', a root position chord. A '6' alone implies that the 3rd is to be played as well as the 6th, forming a first inversion chord, while a '6' and a '4' together thus indicate a second inversion chord. Some basses (especially in the seventeenth century) are largely unfigured. The player is expected to judge what chords are intended, although here again there were conventions: for example, most notes with a sharp in front of them imply a '6' (first inversion) chord.

- For practical reasons, the figuring showing a sharp sign alone (with no number) usually means 'use the major 3rd' (even for example for a bass note C, where the major 3rd is E natural), whereas a flat sign alone means 'use the minor 3rd' (even above a bass D, where the minor 3rd is F natural). This curious convention, unsettling at first, turns out to be particularly helpful in vocal music since it makes transposition much easier. Singers like to transpose today just as much as they did in the Baroque period.

The bass line is played with the left hand, usually in unison with another bass instrument such as the cello (and double bass in orchestral contexts), bass viol or bassoon. In German and French Baroque music the accompaniment should usually be added in the right hand, in three-note chords so as to make complete four-part harmony. Italian practice tended to favour fuller chords in both hands, partly owing to the difference of sonority of Italian harpsichords and partly to provide more dynamic effects.

Players have the discretion, within stylistic limits, to decide on the exact nature and position of the right-hand chords. They may also add, in appropriate circumstances, a certain amount of ornamentation, melodic material, motivic figuration or arpeggiation of the chords. The reason the composers did not indicate these elements is a highly practical one, which is just as valid today as it was in the Baroque period. The notation of figured basses fixes what needs to be fixed (the actual harmonies used for the accompaniment), but it leaves free what may remain free (the way these chords are played) so that players can adapt and adjust their accompaniments to the circumstances of the performance. Musical textures in good, stylish accompaniments need to be varied or adjusted according to four factors:

- the nature of the music itself – an Italian Allegro for violin and a French Adagio for flute need different kinds of accompaniment;
- the instrument used – harpsichord, organ, clavichord and piano all use quite different styles of accompaniment;
- the strength of the instrument or voice that is being accompanied – a Baroque flute or a quiet singer can easily be drowned out by a style of accompaniment appropriate for a violin or a larger instrumental group;
- the acoustic of the room in which the performance takes place – thinly textured accompaniment and quiet stops on an organ can carry much more in a church than would the same accompaniment on a harpsichord.

Many modern editions of Baroque sonatas, chamber pieces and songs include a written-out ('realized') part for the keyboard. Editorial continuo parts are, at best, only a preliminary guide. Many of them, especially in editions dating from before about 1970, are unstylish and either too heavy in texture (the worst ones have the bass line doubled in octaves or full chords that are too heavy) or too elaborate (for example, with a melodic right-hand part changing the fundamental texture: a sonata for solo violin and bass, say, should not be transformed into a trio sonata). Players need not play such editorial parts too faithfully. If they have no doubt about which chords to use they may always play their own versions. At first they might simply vary the editorial right-hand part; then they could attempt something simple yet different by reading just from the figures. Good editions always include the original figures, and the best scholarly ones completely omit editorial realizations.

Learning to read the figures will always lead, eventually, to a better style of accompaniment. The four golden rules for beginners are to make sure:

- that the left hand remains rhythmically stable;
- that the right hand does not move about too much;
- that the accompaniment is not placed too high on the keyboard;
- that when the right hand does move it is as often as possible in the opposite direction to the left hand. This last rule, contrary motion, is perhaps the most important.

Counterpoint

Baroque players generally grouped solo keyboard pieces into three stylistic categories, each of which had separate subcategories. First, there are the styles in strictly contrapuntal polyphonic writing, associated with fugues. Although in such works performers must certainly express the horizontal nature of the melodic lines in all voices, keyboard polyphony derives a powerful harmonic strength from the verticality of chords that can be formed by voices that coincide rhythmically. The strictest contrapuntal styles, as in the seventeenth-century fantasia and ricercar, are usually written in *alla breve* notation (¢), with two or four minims to a bar. This does not mean such works should be played slowly; in fact the quavers should be at the same speed as the semiquavers in normal ¢ time. The style of writing is similar to that of Renaissance vocal polyphony (see, for example, Ex. 3.3). Such works rarely have many ornaments.

Ex. 3.3. J. S. Bach, *Das wohltemperirte Clavier* Book 2, *c.*1740, autograph score: first page of Fugue in E major.

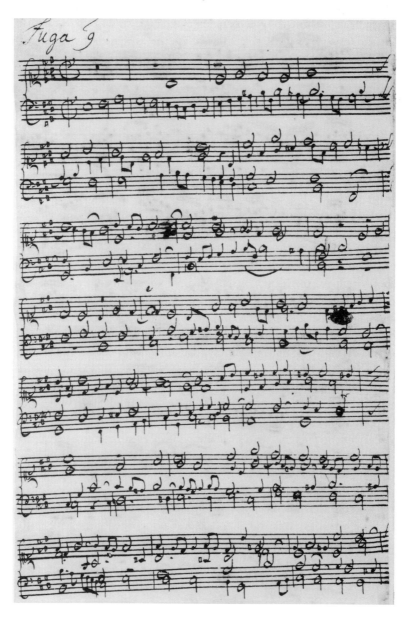

Less vocal and perhaps less severe in style is the equally impressive polyphony found in capriccios. These works are written in faster note-values, but the time signature (**c**) implies a moderate tempo, despite the presence of semiquavers. Capriccios also have few ornament signs, but ornamental figures are more often written into the music.

Counterpoint has something of a reputation for dryness, which is based on a misunderstanding. In the hands of the greatest contrapuntists such as Byrd or Bach, keyboard counterpoint can be one of the most rewarding kinds of music. At its best, the distinctions between 'melody' and 'accompaniment' disappear, since all melodic material is destined at some point to become accompaniment and all the accompaniment figures can become primary melodic phrases. Counterpoint may be seen as a musical equivalent of sculpture. Just as when you walk behind a three-dimensional statue what was the right-hand side becomes the left-hand side, so in counterpoint a bass can become a soprano, and a soprano a bass. A statue looks similar and yet different when seen from the left or right, or from the back; in a similar way, themes can take on different characters depending on whether they stand out as a soprano, fill in the music as an alto or tenor, or support the whole texture as a bass.

Good counterpoint depends on the combination of different melodic figures (as in the subject and countersubject of a Bach fugue), usually characterized by distinct rhythmic figures and phrase lengths. Yet the various themes on which fantasias, ricercars, capriccios and fugues are constructed really only form the substructure that supports such works. They are the part of the composition that is unchanging. On the other hand, different appearances of the themes are often clothed in new counterpoints, invented freshly by the composer for each phrase. While performers need to pay attention to the themes while practising, in fact these will usually be clearly heard by listeners as long as they are clearly understood by the players. For both performers and listeners it can be more musically satisfying to pay attention to the ever-changing new counterpoints that bring fresh life to the texture. This can easily be understood when practising a fugue by actually omitting all the notes that belong to the theme and playing only the unthematic counterpoint. It then becomes clear that beautiful imitative polyphony derives much strength from this 'flesh' around the thematic 'skeleton'.

Dances

The second main category of Baroque keyboard music comprises the various dances found in suites. Of these the most common are the allemande, courante, sarabande and gigue. In eighteenth-century works these four movements are in alternating tempos: slow, fast, slow, fast. (In some seventeenth-century suites, the gigue should follow the allemande.) Each of these dances exists in different varieties. The slow French-style allemandes should never be hurried, despite being written mostly in semiquavers. They are more common than the lighter and faster kind of allemande, written mostly in quavers. The French courante is written with irregular phrase lengths, notated mostly in quavers, with elaborate ornamentation in the right hand, and a characteristically unsettling combination of bars

Ex. 3.4. J. H. d'Anglebert, *Pieces de clavecin*: first page of Sarabande grave.

in 3/2 and 6/4. The Italian *corrente*, on the other hand, is faster, more regular, less ornamented and usually notated in semiquavers. Seventeenth-century sarabandes are usually fast. By the eighteenth century, however, the slower style of French sarabande (Ex. 3.4), with rich chords and elaborate ornamentation, had become common, although a sweeter, more melodic kind also exists (for example, the Aria of Bach's Goldberg Variations). The two basic kinds of gigue were also French and Italian, the former in jerky dotted rhythms, the latter in fast flowing triplets. The English jig is different again (albeit closer to the Italian *giga*). Even the French gigue, with its typical dotted rhythms and steady pace, had a faster version (the *canaries*) and a slower version (the *loure*).

Most of the other movements in keyboard suites (minuets, gavottes, passepieds, chaconnes, etc.) are based on well-known French court dances. Although there is a great variety of such kinds of works, there was a rather precise understanding at the time of what the speed should be for each dance. Taking a Purcell or Froberger sarabande, which should be played quite fast, at the same speed as a slow sarabande by Bach would be a stylistic mistake. In fact, not paying enough attention to composers' expectations concerning tempo is a common error. Froberger, Purcell, Couperin, Rameau, Bach, Handel and all their contemporaries did not need to indicate the speed of dances by an absolute system (such as, later, metronome markings), and often did not even need to use a vaguer indication such as 'allegro' or 'presto', since everyone knew precisely what the speed of each dance should be. The absence of tempo indications is thus certainly not an invitation to modern performers to be free, or to exercise their personal choice in the matter. The title of the dance, along with its style, is usually a clear and specific indication of the precise tempo. It is a grave error of style not to respect this.

On the other hand, players do have considerable liberty, especially in seventeenth-century pieces, when it comes to adding ornamentation on the repeats. Elegant playing of French-style suites often requires the addition of at least some ornaments that are not notated in the score. Each great composer had his own recognizable style of ornamentation, and it is hard to give generalized rules. Some, such as d'Anglebert, Louis Marchand, Couperin and Bach, particularly liked rather dense ornamentation, but many of these ornaments are intimately linked with ways of making the harpsichord sound richly and expressively. They do not translate well on to the organ or piano. Other composers, such as Chambonnières, Lebègue and Handel, seemed to have favoured less heavily ornamented textures. The individual preferences of each composer should ideally be assessed before deciding how much ornamentation to use, and where to add it.

The word 'ornament' implies an embellishment of the music; in other words, the ornaments must make it even more beautiful. The most important notes in the phrase are the obvious candidates to receive particular attention, and the longer notes can have longer ornaments. However, sometimes a more inventive melodic phrase in shorter notes may be used (such passages were known in England as 'divisions'). Certainly, simply adding a few little trills to any convenient notes cannot be considered a sufficient answer to this challenge. (See Chapter 2 'Notation and Interpretation', pp. 30–31 and 43–7 for more general information on dances and ornamentation.)

There is another aspect of Baroque playing which developed as a way of making both harpsichords and organs expressive but can be useful also to pianists. Ornaments need to be varied not only in their length but above all in their speed and intensity. Trills that are uniformly rapid, drilling little holes in the music like road workers or dentists, will never help pianists achieve the elegance and beauty that good harpsichordists can express by using trills of varying speeds and lengths. Frescobaldi says quite specifically, as early as 1615, that longer trills must start slowly, get faster, and slow down again as they end. (Speeding up a trill is quite easy but slowing it down evenly can be much more difficult.) Such trills were used throughout the Baroque period.

The 'fantastic style'

The third main category of Baroque keyboard music is the one in which the player has the greatest freedom. It was known in the seventeenth century as the 'fantastic style', and is best seen in Frescobaldi's and Froberger's wonderful toccatas (Ex. 3.5); the extraordinary French unmeasured preludes by Louis Couperin and d'Anglebert (some of Purcell's preludes are in this style, too); or such later works as Bach's Chromatic Fantasia and Fugue. Some pieces by Froberger are marked with the French words 'à discrétion', meaning that players are expected to take considerable liberty with the time values. François Couperin is more specific: in such pieces 'the imagination gives itself up to whatever comes to mind' and one must not pay too much attention to strictness of time or tempo.

Such music is a sort of kaleidoscope, with different sections (often quite short) alternating slow music with fast, loud with soft, contrapuntal with chordal, consonant with dissonant, and so on. It is usually a good idea here to try and exaggerate the effect the composer has created. The faster passages should be pushed forward in a headlong outpouring of musical energy, while the slower sections should be held back by really putting the brakes on, as much as the circumstances, the instrument or the acoustic in which you are playing will allow. It is a common mistake to play the brilliant fast sections too slowly and the sonorous slow sections too fast.

The organ literature is particularly rich in such pieces, especially among the works of Lübeck, Buxtehude, Böhm and Bruhns. Bach's famous Toccata and Fugue in D minor is a classic example. The organ, naturally, is able to exaggerate all the differences, and you can use the resonance in a church to excellent effect in the pauses between sections (which are also useful for changing stops). Yet many of the seventeenth-century works in the 'fantastic style', for example the toccatas of Frescobaldi, Michelangelo

Ex. 3.5.
G. A. Frescobaldi, *Toccate e partite d'intavolatura di cimbalo* (1615): first page of Toccata prima. The double clef on the left-hand stave shows *f* on the fourth line up and middle C on the sixth.

Rossi, Froberger and Georg Muffat, as well as some 'voluntaries' by English composers such as John Blow, can be played equally well on any keyboard instrument. Bach's seven toccatas that are supposedly for harpsichord mostly use the same style; they are in fact very much at home on the organ (and have been successfully recorded that way). Organists approaching such a free-wheeling work will tend to see it in two ways. Certainly, they will see the instrument as a means of playing the composer's piece, of bringing to life the musical ideas. Yet they will also see the composition as a means of playing the instrument, or showing off what the organ can do. A good performance will be doing both at the same time: the performer uses the instrument to play the piece and uses the piece to play the instrument.

The same is true of many other works, on other instruments. It is in such 'fantastic style' pieces (and there are several in *Das wohltemperirte Clavier*) that pianists may be allowed some special liberties, similar to those enjoyed by organists. Most Baroque keyboard music is restricted to about four octaves in the middle of the piano keyboard. When Bach goes up to his highest note and down to his lowest note, these are the very top and very bottom notes on the harpsichord. And they sound like it, to wonderful effect. Yet on the piano they inevitably have a much weakened effect for the simple reason that such 'extreme' notes are still in the middle of the seven-octave keyboard. The vigorous sensation, so clear on a harpsichord, of Bach – or Rameau, Couperin, Handel and Scarlatti – pushing at the outer limits and stretching the instrument and its player to their fullest capacities can never be successfully created on a piano, and any attempt to do so will sound artificial. While a piano can perfectly well play Bach's ideas in an effective musical way, Bach's music can never play the piano itself as effectively as it can play a harpsichord.

So can a pianist playing Baroque music do anything to make the piano itself speak with its full range of sonorities, more like the piano used by Debussy or Brahms? Whereas it would nowadays be considered inadvisable to add octaves to thematic entries in the bass of a fugue (as Czerny did in his edition of *Das wohltemperirte Clavier*, based on how Beethoven apparently played these works), nevertheless I think pianists who have carefully thought about the 'fantastic style' could sometimes successfully adapt such works in an adventurous and inventive manner. Brahms understood the nature of the problem perfectly. His arrangement of Bach's great violin Chaconne in D minor is for the left hand alone; it thus maintains the strong sensation in the original of going far beyond the normal capacities of the medium. Liszt and Busoni's transcriptions of the same work take a different view, paying less attention to this aspect.

Perhaps the greater historical awareness of Baroque styles that has come about in recent years could now once again encourage pianists to use Bach's music – as well as that of Buxtehude, Bruhns, Böhm and Lübeck, for example, and even Froberger – to explore the full range of their own keyboard in precisely those works that are composed in the 'fantastic style', intended as virtuoso show-pieces for player and instrument.

At any rate, while there are fortunately fewer and fewer people now who continue to find any interest in the rather sterile debate about the relative merits of 'modern' or 'historical' instruments, there is an increasing number of pianists who have become aware that their own instrument is already an 'old' one, already often referred to as an 'acoustic piano'. For many people who rarely listen to classical music, it is already associated with an 'old' repertoire, much of which is over 200 years old. In the twenty-first century the concert grand piano will inevitably be increasingly associated primarily with concerts of 'classical' music, that is, 'early music' of the nineteenth and early twentieth centuries. Electronic keyboards have already fully established themselves in musical life in much the same way that the piano displaced the harpsichord 200 years ago, or that the harpsichord displaced the lute some hundred years before that.

Strings

Andrew Manze

Is it not strange that sheeps' guts should hale souls out of men's bodies?
(Shakespeare, *Much Ado about Nothing*, Act 2, scene iii)

Stringed instruments have been used ever since mankind discovered that sweet music could be made by stretching cords over a resonating chamber and setting them in motion by plucking or bowing. By 1600 most 'stringed' instruments, as we know them, had evolved into forms we still recognize today. Although the violin family takes pride of place in this chapter, since alone of all families it has been at the heart of the repertoire for 400 uninterrupted years, nevertheless many of the principles below apply equally to all stringed instruments.

In the late 1500s the violin family was fully evolved, in terms of its design, well before any repertoire was specifically composed for it. In this respect it was well behind the harp, guitar and lute, which already had their own performing traditions and repertoires in the Renaissance. There was also a plethora of other instruments played *da braccia* ('on the arm') or *da gamba* ('on the leg'), such as the viola d'amore and the viol, with up to seven playing strings and sometimes as many 'sympathetic' strings to resonate gently with the harmony. The violin family was more numerous in the seventeenth century than it is today, with a wide variety of sizes, from 'piccolo' violins to enormous violas, from tiny cellos to massive violones. By 1700 most makers, players and composers had settled on the quartet of instruments we use today, each with four strings: violin, viola, violoncello and double bass. These bore a strong family resemblance, sharing not only the principles upon which they were built but also those by which they were played. In fact many of the comments below about one of the family can be applied to any of the others. Only the double bass still betrays the presence of viol 'genes' in its pedigree, with its sloping shoulders, and the underhand bow hold still used by some players today.

A new Baroque violin

Let us step back in time to the Amati workshop in Cremona in 1600. The air is heavy with the scent of wet varnish and wood dust. There, lying on a bench, is a newly completed violin. At first sight it looks little different from a new violin today: there are the same distinctive outline, *f*-holes, scroll and purfling. Taking a closer look, we see that the bridge is of a simpler design and is smaller, so that the strings are closer to the belly, and the fingerboard is much shorter, leaving more of the belly exposed. A standard 'modern' fingerboard reaches notes two and a half octaves above the open string.

This original fingerboard probably covered little more than an octave – 4th position rather than 14th!

Other differences are harder to see but no less crucial. The neck is shorter and fatter than normal, and it joins the body at a different angle. A 'modern' neck leans back a few degrees, to increase the tension of the strings over the bridge. A 'Baroque' neck is straighter, so that the strings and bridge are under less tension. More tension means more sound. As concert halls, audiences, orchestras and pianos became larger in the later nineteenth century, so more decibels were needed, hence more tension. With it, however, came the risk of the belly collapsing under the strain, so makers reinforced the belly by fitting a longer, thicker bass bar. This strip of wood is visible only by peering through the left *f*-hole; it runs parallel with the strings inside the belly, under the left foot of the bridge. For 'our' violin though, high tension lies far in the future, well after the end of the Baroque era.

The fingerboard and bridge will have to be changed before long. During the seventeenth and eighteenth centuries, bridges became larger and more ornate, as much to reflect the maker's skill as to improve the sound. New styles of bridge are attributed to, among others, Stradivarius and Tartini, a player who was passionate about acoustics. The fingerboard was lengthened to cope with the demands of the more pioneering players who were starting to explore its upper slopes. In 1600 the highest note in regular use on a violin was c''' (i.e. the 4th finger extending a semitone out of 1st position), but by 1700 increasingly adventurous players had reached a''' (in 7th position – the highest note Bach wrote). After 1700, makers gave up fitting fingerboards long enough for the likes of Locatelli, who reached 22nd position, and Vivaldi, who, according to one eyewitness, improvised a cadenza that went so high there was scarcely enough room between his fingers and the bridge for the bow.

Fig. 4.1. Baroque violin (above) and modern violin.

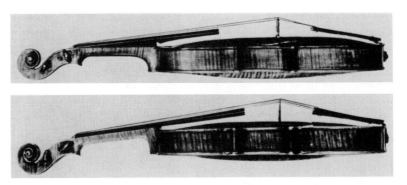

The strings of our 1600 violin are made of gut, highly twisted for strength and density of sound. Gut was in constant use from the earliest times until the twentieth century. It was not taken from cats, as is popularly thought, but from sheep (as Shakespeare well knew), and there were many types, including the confusingly named catline. Most are made by twisting together several strands of gut very tightly, sometimes including a thread or particles of metal. Compared to gut, modern metal strings are louder, brighter and, not surprisingly, more steely in character. Gut strings are softer and more flexible, but they have a shorter life expectancy and are far more sensitive to the variables of climate. High temperatures and humidity, which are as common in modern concert halls as they were in Baroque churches and theatres, make gut strings drop in pitch, while cold and dry conditions make them rise. The twentieth-century violin pedagogue Ivan Galamian, no doubt recalling his own childhood experiences of gut, wrote: 'One should be able to play *in tune* on a violin which is *out of tune*'. Playing in tune is not only a question of knowing where to place each finger, but also of sensing at what pitch the string is and adjusting your fingers accordingly. The player must beware of relying on open strings in case they are out of tune: you should always have a 'plan B' fingering in case of atmospheric difficulties.

The pitch of individual notes changes not only with the weather but also according to the temperament used. Playing in tune with a piano in equal temperament, or with a harpsichord or organ in an unequal temperament or mean-tone, requires a flexibility of the mind as well as the fingers. The art of good intonation is therefore a fascinating and sophisticated one when playing Baroque music. (See Chapter 2 'Notation and Interpretation', p. 23.)

Apart from the difference in sound between gut and metal, there is an appreciable difference in 'feel' when bow touches string. Try stringing your instrument with gut, to experience this difference. At first the gut may seem coarse and imperfect. Before long, though, the simple act of drawing a bow stroke can feel more interesting, as you detect every barb of the bow hair and every microscopic blip on the string's surface. Comparing gut and metal strings is like comparing a candle to an electric light bulb: enjoy both for their distinctive qualities.

Out of the workshop

Our violin would probably have been sold quite easily and for a good price, since Cremonese instruments already had a fine reputation. If it was lucky it might have lived in a wooden case, though probably not one with a folding lid like today's. Most cases opened at one end: the instrument and bow were slid in like a sword into its scabbard. If a violin was less lucky, it might have been transported in a leather bag or just tucked into a coat pocket, and at home it probably hung on the wall. No wonder most old instruments have cracks and scratch marks: they were to be heard, not admired as antiques!

Our violin will have been played in the home and in churches, theatres, town halls and the ballrooms or dining-rooms of the local aristocracy, often the major source of professional employment. There were not yet special-ized concert halls, and so there were few public concerts as we know them. House concerts and the Baroque equivalent of 'jam sessions' at the local tavern no doubt took place, with amateurs and professionals passing an evening in friendly (one hopes) competition. At first, our violin accom-panied singing and dancing (though never in church) or supported vocal groups, filling in any missing voices. There was no solo repertoire and most composers were unfussy about which instruments played what, until 1610.

1610 and all that

1610 was a momentous year for debuts: not just that of Galileo and his new-fangled telescope, or Monteverdi's famous Vespers, the first master-piece of *il nuove musiche*, the 'new' (i.e. Baroque) music. Most important to string players was the debut of the violin as a solo instrument. In Milan, Giovanni Paolo Cima published the first sonatas, in the modern sense of the word, for two, three and four string instruments with basso continuo. The first sonata opens with a pregnant phrase for unaccompanied violin (Ex. 4.1), suggestive of great things to come in the next centuries (Schumann, Brahms, Debussy?).

Ex. 4.1. G. P. Cima, Six Sonatas (1610): Sonata No. 1, opening.

The decades after 1610 saw a proliferation of solo and ensemble pieces written for the church (*da chiesa*) or 'chamber' (*da camera*, i.e. for secular venues and occasions). There were sonatas, canzonas, ricercars, toccatas and, above all, dances of all types. Aristocratic patrons, rich clergy and affluent town councils started to maintain ensembles of musicians with the same pride and enthusiasm that filled their buildings with paintings and their shelves with books. Music still accompanied their singing, dancing and worship, but it also elevated their souls, as well as their social standing. More musicians meant higher elevation, and thus were born orchestras and their music: concerti grossi, dance suites and solo concertos.

Italy produced not only the best string instruments but also the most innovative players. Both spread rapidly throughout Europe, influencing all the musicians and makers they encountered. Itinerant Italians spread the 'new' music: Carlo Farina to Germany, Biagio Marini to Belgium, Lully to France, Pandolfi to Austria, Matteis to England, and many more. Around 1700, largely thanks to publishing houses, some player-composers became internationally famous, enjoying what we might today call 'star attrac-tion'. Arcangelo Corelli, dubbed by his admirers 'a new Orpheus for our times', chose 1 January 1700 as an appropriate date to signal the dawn of a new musical era by publishing his epoch-making Op. 5 sonatas. 'While he played', wrote one observer, 'it was usual for his countenance to be distorted, his eyes to become as red as fire and his eyeballs to roll as in an agony'. He sounds much like the Baroque equivalent of a pop star. Some virtuosos, such as Vivaldi and Tartini, stayed at home, besieged by people wanting to hear them or study with them. Others, such as F. M. Veracini, Locatelli, Geminiani and Mascitti, chose to travel, starting a tradition which was to continue with the likes of Viotti and Paganini in the nine-teenth century, and Carmignola and Accardo in the twentieth.

Although many of the leading players contributed to the rapid advance in virtuosity, their technical tricks were at first merely a means to an end, not an end in themselves. Every art work produced during the Baroque era, however ornate and beautiful, had a simple function at heart. Sonatas were mainly used in two places, as their *da chiesa* and *da camera* epithets suggest. During church services they replaced vocal motets, on the one hand to give the singers a break, on the other to provide the members of the congregation with wordless music as an accompaniment to their own meditations and prayers. In homes, whether private or stately, sonatas provided musical entertainment for participants and audience alike. Before long, composers were revelling in the fact that instrumental pieces, being played (*son-ata*) rather than sung (*cant-ata*), were necessarily free of an explicit storyline or moral message. This gave the composers free rein to indulge in new harmonies and rhythms, and to put new techniques to expressive use. Some theorists called this avant-garde style the *Stylus phantasticus*, since it was born of man's fantasy (see Chapter 3 'Keyboard', pp. 63–5). New techniques ranged from the simplest of slurs and double stoppings to advanced chordal playing, virtuosic bow strokes and *scordatura* (retuning the strings to change the sound and chordal possibilities of the instrument).

In the Baroque era there was hardly any such thing as a full-time composer: most pieces were written by players who composed rather than composers who could play. As a result, they incorporated their own technical strengths and innovations in their music, which became increasingly virtuosic. Through the seventeenth century there was a proliferation of trills (often bowed separately rather than slurred) and finger-twisting runs of semiquavers (known as *perfidia*, 'treachery'). As the repertoire became harder and the range of notes needed increased, how to hold the instrument became an issue.

Fig. 4.2. Louis-Michel Vanloo (1707–71), *Spanish Concert*.

Holding the instrument

Before 1610, and before the need for position shifting, the violin and viola were rested against the ribs, and held in place by the left hand and the downward pressure of the bow. As players shifted higher, so the violin was gradually elevated, until by the mid-seventeenth century it rested on or just below the collar bone. So far, the player's chin had never made contact with the instrument, so there was no need for any pads or rests to be attached to it. (Pads and rests were nineteenth-century, post-Baroque inventions.) Players worked out how to keep the violin safely in position while the left hand shifted up and down. For a long time this was done by choosing clever fingerings with strategically placed open strings, while the left-hand thumb and fingers 'walked' up and down the fingerboard. Provided that the thumb and fingers never moved simultaneously, the violin was always safe from a perilous drop.

Cellists were free of this worry, although spikes were not regularly used until the twentieth century. Players would either rest the instrument on the floor or a stool, or support it on the calves of their legs, with feet slightly splayed if necessary, like a viola da gamba player. It is well worth the 'modern' cellist experimenting without a spike. Once over the initial strangeness, you may experience a not unpleasant freedom and control of the instrument, as it is cradled by your body like an extra limb, rather than anchored to the floor.

On chinlessness

Among *da braccia* players, a debate has long raged about the use of the chin. Purists rightly point out that certain repertoire, notably early French, English and Italian music, was played *senza* chin. More pragmatic players argue that, since vaster tracts of repertoire were played with the chin, it is unrealistic in this day and age to specialize in such a restrictive technique as 'chin-off'. Many 'historically informed' violinists nowadays cover such a wide repertoire that any one, exclusive technique becomes rather a luxury. The debate is not new: one of Biber's colleagues, J. J. Prinner, was moved to write in 1677:

> If you want to play the violin properly you must hold the instrument
> firmly with your chin, otherwise it would be impossible to play quick
> passages which go high then low [i.e. shift quickly]. Nevertheless, I have
> known virtuosi of repute who put the violin against the chest, thinking it
> looks nice and decorative, because they have taken it from a painting
> where an angel is playing to St Francis and found it more picturesque: but
> they should have known that the painter was more artful with his paint-
> brush than he would have been with a violin bow.

It is certainly a worthwhile exercise to try playing without the chin, to experience something of the feeling of these pioneering Baroque violinists. One very positive result is that your head is freer to move, to look around, and perhaps even to think. Players interested in a wider repertoire than the early Baroque might be well-advised not to bother beyond the experimental stage.

Fig. 4.3. Portrait of Francesco Maria Veracini engraved by J. June after F. F. Richter, published in 1744 as frontispiece to *Sonate accademiche* Op. 2. The carefully posed portrait shows a chin-off posture with the violin resting on the collar bone rather than the shoulder.

The chin debate, whichever outcome we favour, has important implications for fingering. Playing for a few minutes without the chin will quickly reveal that 1st position is not difficult. So use 1st position as often as possible without embarrassment. Baroque composers were expecting it, and did not try to make life unnecessarily hard for the players. It was not in their interests: published music had to look, as well as be, within the customer's capabilities, or else it would not sell, and professional performances had to sound well, often with little rehearsal. Turnover of repertoire was fast, since the music-buying public and the local employers wanted a constant supply of new works, and musical fashions changed as quickly as in today's pop music. So there was no point in a composer frightening his customers or his colleagues with unplayable difficulties. There are of course exceptions. Some publications were in effect a technical manifesto or a treatise in music, such as Biber's and Walther's solo works, and Locatelli's *L'arte del violino* with its fiendish *Capricci* that so inspired Paganini. Other works were composed specifically for a few, select players, such as Vivaldi's concertos in manuscript (as oppose to those published) and Bach's unaccompanied sonatas and partitas.

Vibrato

There are other implications of chinlessness. Vibrato is still possible, especially a wrist or finger vibrato, though a full arm vibrato tends to move the whole instrument, to the detriment of bow–string contact. Vibrato was seen as a powerful way to imitate the emotional range of the human voice, and was widely used in the Baroque era, though more by players in a solo role than when playing in orchestras. In their treatises, Tartini, Geminiani and Leopold Mozart all refer to the different effects of changing the speed and width of vibrato, and disagree only about how much it should be used. Geminiani's opinion is that 'it may be made on any note whatsoever', while Mozart chides players who constantly wobble 'as if they had the palsy'. What all writers agree on is that vibrato is most useful on long notes, equal in rank to an ornament such as a trill or grace note. As with all ornaments, it should be used with care. Think of it as a cooking spice, and decide for yourself how spicy you like your music.

Fingering

As we saw earlier, chinlessness means that shifting up is not much of a problem but shifting back down is. This fact alone can often suggest a fingering of convenience which turns out not only to be authentic but also to have positive musical implications. Bach's Ciaccona provides a good example:

Ex. 4.2. J. S. Bach, Sonatas and Partitas for violin, 1720: Partita No. 2 in D minor BWV 1004, Ciaccona, bb. 56–61.

If the upper fingering might be termed 'modern' (it appears in several twentieth-century editions of Bach), the lower fingering is perhaps more 'authentic', meaning that it is arguably the one the majority of eighteenth-century players would have chosen. Shifting up to the *e′′′* in bar 56 is a simple affair both with a chin rest and without using the chin at all. Shifting back down for the following *g′′*, however, is far more complicated without the chin, involving a deft left hand. Staying up in 4th position and walking down one position at a time during the next four bars is not only a more practical solution, but it also has an important, musical implication: it creates the illusion that the violin is polyphonic, literally 'having many voices'. Violinists will see straightaway that the lower fingering makes a regular string pattern for the sequence starting in bar 57. The impression given is that there are four 'voices', each with its own string, which all appear in bars 60 and 61.

In the Baroque era, as well as there being a far richer cornucopia of string instruments in regular use than is the case today, there was a wide diversity in the pitches used, from country to country, from town to town, and sometimes within one ensemble. Bach often had to score his cantatas for instruments in two or three different pitches playing simultaneously. One player's A was maybe another's C or F♯. The string maker simply produced gut of a certain length and thickness for every type of instrument, from a *contrabasso* to a *mandolino*. He cared not a jot what you actually called its pitch. To avoid confusion, the four strings of a violin, viola and cello were called (in ascending order) *basso*, *tenore*, *canto* (literally the 'singer') and *cantino* (the 'little singer'), or variants on these names: the French term *chanterelle* is a straight translation of *cantino*, while the German equivalent, *Chorsaite*, is a more general 'choral string'. Knowing this can open up a whole new way of looking at your instrument when playing Baroque music: it no longer has just one voice but is potentially a miniature string quartet.

Unfortunately, it's rare for composers to use these string names to tell us what fingering they have in mind. Vivaldi wrote one concerto (RV 243) to be played entirely *senza cantino*, and occasionally gave fingerings elsewhere. A good example is to be found in the 'Four Seasons'. Although this is one of the most famous works in the Baroque repertoire, Vivaldi's own fingering is rarely heard as the 'Summer' cuckoo rises:

Ex. 4.3. A. Vivaldi, *Il cimento dell'armonia e dell'inventione* Op. 8 (1725): Concerto No. 2 *L'estate*, first movement, bb. 31–40. Vivaldi's implied fingering is shown in square brackets below the stave. In practical terms, 'tutto sopra il Canto' indicates that the upper notes should be played on the A and not the E string; the E string is to be used from b. 39.

Il Cucco

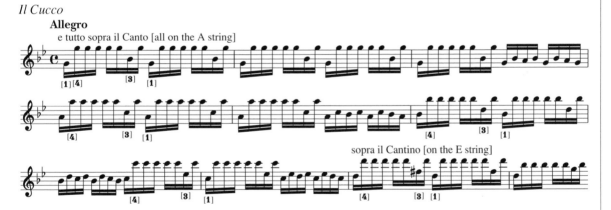

On the cello, because fingerboard distances are so much greater, the range of notes which can be covered by the left hand is smaller. This rules out some polyphonic fingerings, however attractive the idea. Cellists must think polyphonically and create a multi-voice illusion even when the fingering blurs the edges between those voices. Take Bach's solo suites: we do not know how well the composer played the cello, if he did at all, but can be fairly certain that he played the violin and viola far better. It's therefore not surprising that, when the cello suites are played on the viola an octave higher, or the violin a 12th higher, many 'polyphonic' fingerings become possible.

Once you have started to think polyphonically, there is no end to the delights and discoveries in store. Baroque music is full of two- and three-voice conversations and arguments, even when the relationship between strings and fingering is not as tidy as described above. (Exx. 4.6 and 4.8–12 below all contain conversations of some sort.) Here are three voices at the start of a Telemann fantasia, first in its original form and then showing its implied polyphony:

Ex. 4.4.
G. P. Telemann,
Twelve Fantasias for
violin (1735): No. 12
in A minor, first
movement,
Moderato, bb. 1–4
(a) original notation;
(b) possible
reconstruction of
'polyphony'.

The bow

However great its player or maker, any violin is silent without its bow, often described as 'the soul of the violin'. Unlike the violin, the bow was constantly evolving during the Baroque era. Sadly, while many violin makers are now world-famous, we know the names of few bow makers. In 1600, bows were only about half the size of their modern descendants, in terms of length, weight and the number of hairs. By 1750, after a process of constant experimentation, they had grown longer, heavier and hairier, but without losing their most distinctive feature: the stick always curved outwards, away from the hair, Robin Hood-style.

The bow hold was at first very different from today's. The thumb was placed under the frog, and the fourth finger under, rather than on, the stick. This fairly primitive technique has sometimes been used as evidence that the player changed the hair's tension, making the bow 'squashier' for chords or 'harder' for single notes. This is a misapprehension which still surfaces today. (Its most infamous child was the so-called 'Bach bow', a German invention of the 1920s which allowed the bow to sustain three- and four-note chords by means of a mechanism to tighten or loosen the hair.) The thumb-under hold was fine for simple, formulaic bowing patterns, but restricting for anything more virtuosic. The first players to abandon it were the top 'sonatists', and once other players saw and heard their improved facility, the old hold was quickly abandoned. It came to be known as the 'French grip' because France was where it survived the longest. Michel Corrette's *L'école d'Orphée* (1738) promotes both holds as equally valid, 'depending on your teacher'.

When you look at many of the pictures of early eighteenth-century violinists, you may notice that the hand holds the stick higher up, further from the frog, than is usual today. This can make the bow feel lighter and thus more dainty, which is very appropriate for some of the gentler music of the late Baroque, although it is limiting when applied to all types of Baroque music. You can capture something of the feel of a Baroque bow simply by holding a modern bow further up the stick than usual. One or two centimetres should be enough for this experiment.

Messa di voce

As a result of the out-curve of the Baroque bow, the hair is furthest from the stick at the middle. A long bow-stroke, made with equal speed and pressure, will start relatively softly, continue with as much depth of sound as you want, or can muster, and end with a natural tailing away. This gentle crescendo and diminuendo is a Baroque bow's most natural and characteristic stroke. Today rather unkindly termed the 'Baroque bulge', in former times it was given the far more charming title *messa di voce*, 'the placing of the voice'. It was considered that such a note mimicked the natural tendency of the greatest of God's instruments, the human voice. As Tartini said, 'Per ben suonare, bisogna ben cantare' (To play well, one must sing well).

The accusation of bulginess is justified when the shaping of notes is not done with sensitivity. In Ex. 4.5 a carefully measured amount of *messa di voce* on each of the long notes can complement perfectly the alternation of concord and gentle discord between the melody and bass.

Largo ma non tanto

Ex. 4.5. J. S. Bach, Concerto in D minor for two violins BWV 1043, 1730–31: second movement, Largo ma non tanto, bb. 1–2, with a simplified bass line.

Articulation

The middle of the bow is the best place for fast notes, because there the bow is light and can get into and out of the string easily, without any special wrist or finger action. When playing the next example with a Baroque bow, you do not need to think about whether the bow stroke is on or off the string, or worry about the endings of notes: the bow naturally takes care of all such things, which we might term 'articulation'.

Vivace

If the *messa di voce* enables music to sing, then articulation is what makes it speak. It is the playing equivalent of clear diction and appropriate punctuation. In Baroque schools, pupils were taught rhetoric, the art of speaking clearly, grammatically and above all persuasively. The bow is the player's oratorical tool: its clarity is achieved through a clear tone, grammar is via phrasing, and persuasion is a case of appropriate characterization and gesture. As Corelli asked his student, 'Non l'intendite parlare?' – 'Do you not hear it speak?'

Ex. 4.6. J. S. Bach, Concerto in D minor for two violins BWV 1043, 1730–31: first movement, Vivace, bb. 1–4.

To translate this ideal into practice, just think how many ways there are to begin a note: probably as many as there are letters in the alphabet. Play Ex. 4.6 on any instrument and try expressing different letters, not just 't' or 'd' but 'b', 'm' and 'f', saving a shapely vowel for the tied *c♮″* (with a tasteful *messa di voce*, of course). Baroque music is at its most powerful when it appears to speak or sing to us. In 1640 one writer, G. B. Doni, remarked: 'Sometimes you can hear accents and words expressed by the violin which truly seem to come from the human mouth'.

Chords

Most treatises from the last 200 years have something to say about how best to play chords. Many of their realizations are valid for Baroque music, such as those in Ex. 4.7:

Ex. 4.7. A few examples of how to spread a chord.

The bass of a chord is supremely important. It defines the nature of the harmony, whether in root position or inversion, and it often shows the harmonic direction of a phrase. Equally important, however, is its *rhythmic* strength: it defines *where* the beat falls. If the cellist of a string quartet were constantly to be ahead of, or behind, the beat, the other members would soon despair. So, on a stringed instrument, with its several 'voices' (*basso, tenore*, etc.), the bass must be on the beat. Or, to put it another way, the bass *is* the beat. Therefore, avoid playing chords upside down. Also beware of holding the second highest note as long as the highest, and thus favouring it unfairly at the expense of the bass. Ex. 4.8 shows three ways of realizing Bach's original notation. The first two are harmonically and rhythmically ungrammatical. Note how the last makes use of the listener's innate ability to remember notes, a 'memory' on which all polyphonic string writing depends.

Ex. 4.8. J. S. Bach, Six Suites for violoncello, *c.*1720: No. 2 in D minor BWV 1008, Courante, bb. 1–3 (a) original notation; (b) three ways of realizing the chord in b. 2, the last of which is the most appropriate.

A useful way to discover the grammar and logic of chordal passages is to play them without the bow, pizzicato. Notice that most chords are in effect upward arpeggios, even if they only have two notes. As every guitarist and harpist knows well, the speed of spreading the arpeggio can be very expressive: anything from very fast, creating the illusion of the notes sounding simultaneously (as in Ex. 4.9), to extremely slow, lingering on every 'voice' (Ex. 4.10).

Rule of down-bow

From the characteristics of early bows and bow hold described above, a system of bowing patterns evolved which is now known as the 'Rule of

Tempo di Borea

Ex. 4.9. J. S. Bach, Sonatas and Partitas for violin, 1720: Partita No. 1 in B minor BWV 1002, Tempo di Borea, bb. 1–4.

Adagio

Ex. 4.10. J. S. Bach, Sonatas and Partitas for violin, 1720: Sonata No. 1 in G minor BWV 1001, first movement, Adagio, b. 1.

down-bow'. This Rule required that in dance music, and most music derived from dance patterns, the first beat of the bar, and every other strong beat or emphatic harmony within the bar, was to be played with a down-bow. Such a rule might seem harsh and unmusical (Geminiani called it 'wretched') until we remember that most of us are naturally right- or left-handed and right- or left-footed. In the same way, the bow has its 'good' and 'bad' strokes. Geminiani himself used these very terms, *buono* and *cattivo*, for down- and up-bow. So the 'Rule' was born of common sense, acknow-ledging the fact that the down-bow is naturally stronger than the up. Admittedly, on *da braccia* instruments gravity plays a large part in helping the down-bow feel more important. On *da gamba* instruments, arm weight is the equivalent of gravity, making a down-bow sound stronger than an up, unless the player compensates.

Since the nineteenth century, players have gone to great lengths to iron out this natural difference, as if ashamed of an in-built design fault. In Baroque times, this 'fault' was put to good advantage. The Rule felt so natural that it did not need enforcing or learning, and for a long time did not even have a name. It makes an appearance not only in every musical example in this chapter but in most Baroque pieces, and was so deeply rooted that its traces survive well into the Romantic era. Early orchestral parts hardly ever have bowings marked in, because the Rule meant that all the players, sharing as they usually did a musical language and repertoire, spontaneously agreed on what bowing and phrasing to do. Imagine how much time this saved. (The lack of markings may also be because pencils were too expensive for mere musicians.)

Slurs

As experiments produced a longer, heavier bow, so players could produce a more cantabile, sostenuto and legato sound. Of course the heavier the bow, the more effort was needed to move it and the slower its maximum speed: so slurs, rather than separate bowing, became more common and elaborate. One anecdote illustrates this step in the bow's evolution. As a young man in Padua, Giuseppe Tartini was already an accomplished violinist, far surpassing his local colleagues in ability. He attended a performance by another virtuoso, Francesco Maria Veracini of Florence, and was so impressed by the latter's bow control that he withdrew from public performance for a year of intense practice. There were two results: *L'arte del arco* (The Art of Bowing), a set of ingenious variations on a gavotte by Corelli; and a longer bow. Veracini's bowing skill can easily be imagined today by looking at how long some of the slurs are in his *Sonate accademiche* Op. 2.

Scordatura

One of the techniques which violinists borrowed from lute and viol players was *scordatura*, literally 'mistuning'. Any or all of the strings are deliberately retuned to enable otherwise impossible chords to be played and to change the instrument's tone. The first Italian to use the technique was Marini, who (in his Op. 8, 1626) requires the player to tune the E string down to *d″* and later back up again in the middle of a sonata. The most imaginative and adventurous exponent of *scordatura* was undoubtedly the Bohemian virtuoso Biber. His fifteen Rosary (or Mystery) Sonatas, depicting the Mysteries of the Virgin Mary, each use a different tuning. The music is notated as if the tuning was normal, so the player must (rather aptly) have faith, playing the notes as they look, rather than as they sound. Ex. 4.11 shows what Biber wrote and how those notes actually sound:

(a)
Tuning

(b)

Ex. 4.11.
H. I. F. Biber,
Rosary Sonatas,
?1676: No. 12, third
movement,
Allamanda, bb. 1–2
(a) original notation;
(b) actual sound.

'Sonate, que me tu veux?'

'Sonata, what do you want of me?' This was the despairing question of French connoisseurs when they first came face to face with the abstract sonatas of the Italians. What are they all about? Although a few pieces are programmatic, representing natural or man-made phenomena such as storms, battles, cuckoos and laments, the vast majority of instrumental works are abstract, in the sense that the composer offers no helping hand in the form of a title, storyline or moral message. Instead there were just the generic titles: sonata, canzona, suite and concerto. Composers probably never dreamed that people would be playing their music 300 years later, with no direct experience of their life and times. As a result, Baroque music as written, and printed, is fairly empty of crucial instructions about tempo, dynamic, expression and overall characterization; and a whole tradition of ornamenting and improvising has vanished, since it was hardly ever notated. The composer trusted the performers to make suitably tasteful decisions. Players could choose their own radically different ways of playing the same piece, musically as well as technically, and all be equally 'correct'. For example, the opening of Corelli's Sonata Op. 5 No. 7 (Ex. 4.12) could be played *forte* with accents, the quavers all staccato, off the string in the middle of the bow, to sound proud and assertive. Or it could be slower, *mezzo-forte*, more legato, on the string in the upper half of the bow, more like a church choir singing a sacred psalm. Or it could equally legitimately be *pianissimo*, *staccatissimo*, at the heel perhaps, a Baroque 'Teddy Bears' Picnic'.

Ex. 4.12. A. Corelli, Twelve Sonatas Op. 5 (1700): No. 7 in D minor, first movement, Preludio, bb. 1–3.

One of the great joys of playing Baroque music is this very absence of instructions about how to play the music, an absence which at first looks like a big problem. We are forced to imagine what Corelli would say to us if he walked into the room. However vast our knowledge of historical performance practice, of Corelli's life and of music in Rome in 1700, we can still only guess what his answer would be to our many questions. His answer to the Op. 5 No. 7 question might well have been: 'I know what I would do, but I don't mind what you do. I've done my part as composer. It's up to you to do yours as the performer'.

Continuo playing

Cellists will often be called upon to play bass lines. This should never be approached as an exercise in mere accompaniment. A bass line performed with intelligence and sensitivity can have a great influence on the rhythm, tempo, momentum, phrasing and overall expression of a piece. In fast movements it can generate great energy by its articulation and accents, while in slower pieces it can hold a regular pulse, around which the solo part can float at will.

Cellists must always be aware of whether their parts are functional bass lines or actively melodic. When the bass is purely functional, it is the equivalent of a building's underground foundations, without which the building would collapse. Foundations, however, should never be the centre of the listener's attention, so use vibrato sparingly and tellingly, to affect expression or add stabbing accents. Or use it to introduce new colours for strange or unexpected bass notes, such as in an interrupted cadence or a shift to the Neapolitan key (a semitone above the tonic).

When bass lines are more melodic, vibrato should be used which matches the solo part (or parts). Melodic bass lines, while still functional, are also ornamental. They are more like a building's columns, which are beautiful to look at *and* essential to keep the roof up. Often the bass part switches frequently within a movement from one type to another, from functional to melodic. One telltale sign of a melodic role is when the bass line imitates, or is imitated by, the treble. Ex. 4.12 is a case in point: rather than merely accompanying the treble, the bass part is an equal partner in a duet.

Often a cello plays basso continuo parts alongside a piano, harpsichord or organ. Remember two things: that these keyboard instruments cannot do vibrato, and that once their notes or chords are struck there is little the player can do to alter the sound. With a piano, a full-bodied cello tone is required, and care should be taken to blend with the piano's sound. The harpsichord, on the other hand, can articulate and accent the start of notes very well, but does not sustain tone as well as a piano. So the cellist should not worry too much about the attack of a note, but should concentrate on shaping the body of the note. The *messa di voce*, which can be graded in a hundred microscopically different ways, is just one of the possible shapes to give a single note. Imagine that each note is a line. Too many straight lines become boring, as do too many bulges. There are many lovely ways to shape a line tastefully, so try to reproduce those shapes with the bow. The organ is almost the opposite of a harpsichord in that it has little power to attack or vary the beginnings of notes, compared to a stringed instrument, but once the note has started it continues with a constant, unwavering tone. The cellist can create a whole variety of articulations and note shapes, and create the illusion that the organ is varying its accents, doing dynamics and phrasing, even at times breathing.

Above all, bass line players must be aware of the main characteristic of Baroque harmony: it shuttles between discord and concord. Every discord must be resolved by a concord, and every discord should therefore be more *x* than its resolving concord, where *x* equals tense, painful, joyful, fruity or whatever your chosen character is at that moment. Harmony is usually indicated by figures written above or below the bass line, which is why a Baroque bass part is sometimes called 'figured bass'. The complete cellist will be able to 'read' these figures, and as a result enjoy and understand the music better. The system is actually very simple to learn, and it shows in numerals where, and how strong, the discords and concords are. For example, a note figured '7' (a 7th chord, always a discord) cries out to be leaned on with more *x* than a note with no figure (which means it is a normal, concordant triad). (See Chapter 3 'Keyboard', p. 58.)

In Baroque times, some cellists even 'realized' their bass lines; that is they harmonized their own bass part. Some were skilful enough to be able to realize the harmony completely unaccompanied, by adding chords or arpeggios. More and more cellists are recreating this technique nowadays. A good way to start trying this is by looking at the chords which Bach used, particularly in his first four cello suites. (The fifth and sixth are less helpful, being written in *scordatura* and for a five-string cello respectively.) Here are some rules of thumb:

- Keep any added chords simple. The vast majority of Baroque harmonies contain just three different notes. Since the bass and melody parts usually provide two of them, there is often only one 'new' note to add, so a double stop is often sufficient.
- Avoid consecutive octaves and 5ths, not just in your own part but between your part and the melody. These were thought to be most unpleasant in Baroque times.
- Resolve any discords, or else the musical 'sentence' may sound unfinished.
- Avoid the 3rd of the chord if it is in the melody part, but add it if it is not. This helps avoid the dreaded consecutives.

The double bass was included in Baroque chamber music more often than in Classical and Romantic and, when played with great sensitivity, can beautifully enhance a basso continuo line.

The harp has yet to reclaim one of its main roles in Baroque music, that of playing basso continuo. For harpists, learning to read figured bass, which is anyway useful for one's harmonic sense, opens up the possibility of accompanying solo, chamber and orchestral repertoire. Seventeenth-century music does not usually stray far in terms of its keys, so there is little pedal work, but it requires great variety of, and sensitivity to, texture and chord voicing.

Hale and farewell

If playing Baroque music sometimes seems rule-bound, take heart from the fact that the words 'free', 'freedom' and 'flexibility' occur far more often in this chapter than 'rule'. Listeners will be happier to hear your own ideas about how to play a piece than a way learnt from a book. Go forth and use those sheeps' guts to hale souls out of bodies!

Stephen Preston

Wind Instruments

The instruments

Probably the most useful thing to know about if you are playing Baroque music on a wind instrument is the difference in construction between instruments of the period and modern instruments. Your instrument is bigger and heavier in every way than its historical counterpart. Being aware of this simple fact and understanding its technical and musical implications can give you a surprising number of valuable insights. What you don't need to be told about period instruments is how primitive they were, how they were inferior to modern instruments, and how Baroque composers, had they heard them, would have much preferred to have their music played by modern instruments. There are many absurdities in these statements. But that doesn't mean that Baroque music can't be played very successfully on modern instruments.

Woodwind

The Baroque oboe, flute and recorder were developed in France during the second half of the seventeenth century. While the development of the bassoon is more obscure, it too probably underwent its most significant changes in France about the same time. The two-keyed Baroque clarinet, however, was first recorded in Germany in 1710. Why was it not cultivated earlier? Compared to the other woodwinds, it presumably lacked the requisite tonal and inflectional qualities. It was these qualities – a warmer tone-colour, dynamic flexibility and less penetrating sound – which made the new Baroque instruments significantly different from their earlier Renaissance forms.

This new Baroque sound was the result of a number of constructional changes which in general produced lighter instruments. In particular, bodies were divided into joints rather than made in a single piece of wood. Finger-holes and bores were made smaller; the bores of the flute and recorder tapered towards the foot. The bells of the oboe and bassoon were more lightly constructed. Additional keywork was added, giving the flute one key, the oboe two and bassoon three. The windway and block of the recorder mouthpiece were made curved rather than straight, allowing greater control of pitch and dynamics.

Horn, trumpet and trombone

Light construction was critical with these three instruments. They had thinner walls, smaller bells, and mouthpieces which offered brilliance,

Fig. 5.1. 'Trumpet' by Johann Christoph Weigel, copper engraving from *Musicalisches Theatrum* (*c*.1722).

clarity and control. The horn and trumpet players needed this control; in the absence of valves, the embouchure did all the work.

The horn was probably developed in its circular form in France in the mid-seventeenth century. Initially, having only one or more fixed coils, it could be played in just one key. Early eighteenth-century modifications allowed for key changes by inserting different length crooks, but the player was still totally dependent on his embouchure and, as with the trumpet, remained confined to the harmonic series (Ex. 5.1, p. 89). Hand-stopping – placing the hand in the bell to produce a complete chromatic scale – was not introduced as a technique until the early Classical period.

The trumpet and trombone hardly changed from the Renaissance to the Baroque period. The natural trumpet consisted simply of two tubes linked to the bell section; but for all its simplicity the solo trumpeter was high in the musical hierarchy and required a phenomenal technique. The trombone, or sackbut as it was called then, was a moderately voiced instrument and as agile as the violin. In the early Baroque period these qualities were reflected in an excellent repertoire, though in the late seventeenth century the instrument went into a period of decline.

Baroque techniques

As you will see, Baroque techniques were much less muscular, more relaxed and more flexible, and allowed greater physical freedom than those of the present day. The following snippets of information should give you useful technical and interpretative insights.

Fig. 5.2. Antoine Watteau, *Man Playing a Flute*, c.1710.

Breath, embouchure and support

Baroque mouthpieces, embouchures and reeds were designed to encourage resonance and flexibility. All Baroque wind instruments required less air than their modern counterparts to resonate in the body of the instrument. Because they spoke more easily, they offered less resistance, and required less effort, volume and intensity of air, while allowing subtle control.

Tone and volume: colour, equality and dynamics

The design of Baroque instruments, especially in the case of the flute, made them quieter than wind instruments are now. In fact trumpeters who specialized in playing solos, sonatas and concertos were praised for their ability to play as quietly as a flute. Because of the difficulty of acquiring and keeping this technique, they were excused duties demanding continuous loud playing. Accompanists were reminded to listen to the soloist or principal part in order not to overpower it.

There was often considerable variation between natural and chromatic notes (the Greek word *khroma* means colour). Adjacent notes were often unequal in tone and volume, depending on the octave they were in and the technique used to produce them. However, unvarying dynamics and complete homogeneity of tone were regarded as unimaginative and boring; contrast and variety were essential. On the woodwinds the fingerings used for chromatic notes resulted in a softer sound, especially in the bottom register. Composers and performers deliberately exploited these 'inequalities', varying volume, colour, articulation and rhythm for expressive effect. Loud playing for its own sake was considered bad musicianship.

Articulation

The ease with which sound could be produced allowed for light, easy articulation: we have already noted the agility of the trombone. Notes could be rhythmically and expressively varied, alternating effortlessly between stronger and weaker, and grading the difference between tonguing and slurring.

Intonation

Although good intonation was more difficult to attain, the responsiveness of the instrument allowed excellent musicians to play with very fine tuning. Depending on the instrument, various techniques were used to control the intonation, including: varying the strength and placement of support within the body; lip control and breath speed; special fingerings; half-covering holes; and covering more or less of the embouchure. These techniques are similar to those required in some contemporary music.

Ornamentation

Because Baroque musicians were physically more in contact with their instruments, with less intervening keywork, ornamentation was generally easier than it is today, although horn and trumpet players required good embouchures to achieve the necessary agility.

Fig. 5.3. 'Waldhorn' (hunting horn) by J. C. Weigel, from *Musicalisches Theatrum.*

Interpretation on modern instruments

There were two main formative influences on Baroque music: dance, its rhythms, structure and performance; and language, its inflections, structures, and the delivery of speech and words.

Bearing this in mind, begin your approach to interpretation by asking questions about the music. If you ask the right questions, look at the possibilities suggested by the music and do a little good reading about performance practice, you are more likely to arrive at a musical result than by assuming your musical instinct and training have given you all you need to know.

The most important question to ask yourself is the most simple. What is the usual word for 'making' music? Of course the answer is obvious: play. Then ask yourself how often does *playing* feel more like *work*? Unfortunately the answer is that all too often playing *is* really hard work. Sometimes the difficulty of a piece is an important element, but this isn't true of most Baroque wind music. On the contrary, it was composed to give delight and pleasure to both performer and listener. Sadly, it's not uncommon to hear Baroque music played with great technical ability but in such a way that the musical meaning and enjoyment stay out of reach. The harder such performers work, the harder their work becomes – and like a dog trying to catch its own tail, they never catch the real music. The solution is to learn to 'work' less and 'play' more. Develop your insight and understanding of what Baroque music was about, how it was played, and what the Baroque version of your instrument was like.

Ex. 5.1. Harmonic series on C, showing the partials present in addition to every fundamental note; their varying proportions create a note's colour. The partials shown in black are out of tune in equal temperament.

Tone

Aim at producing warm, full but light tone-colours. Develop the lower partials in your tone, as the higher even-numbered partials produce a harder edged, more cutting sound. (The partials constitute the fundamental and overtones, or harmonics, of a tone.) Partials 3, 5 and 7 will not only give your sound more warmth and colour, but will also help you blend better with other instruments. Develop a more fluid use of the breath, more flexible support, more relaxed embouchure. With a full but soft-edged sound you can play loudly without being overpowering. If you enjoy playing Baroque music, consider using a special mouthpiece, head-joint or reed to make the production of a warm, flexible tone easier.

Intonation

It might seem odd to think about intonation in relation to modern instruments; after all, isn't it old instruments that are supposed to be out of tune? In fact, your scientifically tuned instrument doesn't have all the advantages – especially as equal temperament was not the standard Baroque tuning system. In the Baroque period a number of different tuning systems were used, but the one aspect which is of musical importance to us now is that sharps were played lower then and flats higher. This is exactly the opposite of what you would expect. Baroque sharps were thought of as tending towards the natural notes of the same name (they 'sharpened' them), and flats also towards the corresponding naturals (they 'flattened' them). For example, A♯ relates to A and is therefore lower in pitch than B♭ which relates to B. Even when played as leading notes, sharps were kept low. The woodwinds used different enharmonic fingerings to reflect these tunings.

Why should you bother with this? Because pieces were composed to be heard with the colour of accidentals enhancing their expression. Equal temperament can sound 'white' or even 'acid' where Baroque intonation sounded coloured and warm. Practise tuning accidentals by listening carefully to the harmony as you play, and pushing the pitch gently up or down (depending on whether the note is a sharp or a flat), until you hear an expressive change of colour without it sounding obviously out of tune.

Dynamics

Baroque winds were quieter than modern instruments, and their tone-colours warmer and less penetrating. However, don't try to imitate a period instrument: this would be as absurd as trying to play an old instrument like a modern one. Develop a tone that is light, bright, round and warm – even when you are playing loudly. Relax your diaphragm so that it can support subtle dynamic changes, agile, lively articulation and easily inflected, swinging rhythms. You can and should use the dynamic potential of your instrument fully, but develop contrast and variety of dynamics within phrases rather than crudely alternating *forte* with *piano*. The key is a relaxed technique. Keep your embouchure, tongue, throat, diaphragm, chest and back free from tightness or rigidity. The same applies to your shoulders, arms, hands and fingers. Think 'open and free'; the more lightly and fluently you can use your muscles the easier you will find the music is to play.

One of the most informative eighteenth-century books on performance was written by Johann Joachim Quantz; it has been translated into English by Edward R. Reilly as *On Playing the Flute*. Don't be put off by its title if you're not a flute player, as it contains a great deal of useful information on a wide variety of subjects including orchestral playing, and some very detailed examples of dynamics. (For one example, see Ex. 2.6 on p. 33.)

Rhythm and articulation

Stravinsky made the observation that most Baroque music was dance music. Much seventeenth- and eighteenth-century repertoire was either specifically written for dancing, composed in the forms and rhythms of particular dances, or strongly influenced by dance. The coincidence of dance-steps with the musical bar emphasized the importance of the downbeat. For example, it is essential in gavottes and other pieces beginning with incomplete bars that the emphasis of the phrase is projected towards the bar line and the downbeat, as this was when the first dance-step was performed. Music- and dance-masters marked time audibly on the downbeat of each bar by beating with hand or foot, which stayed in its lowered position until it was raised in the middle of the bar (in all time signatures divisible by two), or on the last third of the bar (in all triple times). Try beating time in this way: you should feel the polarity of strong and weak between large note divisions and smaller subdivisions. The variation of note weight and length is quite like the swing of jazz and popular music. Even when notated as equal, the notes in Baroque music should rarely be played identically, and sometimes their written rhythmic values should be deliberately altered. (See Chapter 2 'Notation and Interpretation', pp. 36–42.)

To achieve full rhythmic flexibility, learn to change the force and quality of your articulation, varying the weight, relative volume and length of notes. Use a well-supported, very clear, gentle, fluid and fluent articulation. If you aren't supporting your airstream, the tongue can only make a brief explosion of air without tone. When the articulation can't be lightened sufficiently, add slurs, but don't 'blanket' the music in endlessly repetitive slurred patterns. Research Baroque rhythmic alteration and the special articulations used on your instrument to aid rhythmic flexibility. Build your interpretation on the basis that rhythm was always a vital element in performance, and aim at developing a clear stylistic and technical conception of what you're trying to achieve, ideally by working with a musician who can demonstrate practically how it's done. Remember that what you are now trying to do was for Baroque musicians a normal part of technique and interpretation, whereas modern practices, training and instrument technology demand exactly the opposite: complete equality of tone and articulation, and the exact interpretation of the written note-lengths.

Fig. 5.4. Pierre Mignard, *St Cecilia Playing the Harp*, 1691, detail showing recorder and oboe.

Phrasing

Baroque instruction books often compare musicians to actors, musical phrasing to speech, and the expression of notes to the expression of the meaning of words. Consider the many different ways the same speech can be phrased and breath taken, and you will realize the many possibilities there are for phrasing and breathing, even in apparently identical places in the same piece of music. What makes good Baroque phrasing and breathing is the way they are part of the sense *you* make of the music. There are many more exciting possibilities for varied phrasing and breathing than you might have realized from using over-edited modern editions. Bad editions hide the meaning of the music with repetitive, over-complicated slurs, unmusical articulations and dynamics. Baroque performance should be lively and varied, not static and monumental. Treat phrasing, varied articulations and slurs as forms of ornamentation – as a means of enhancing expression according to your current insights but not as your last word on interpretative decisions.

Breathing

How and where you take breath very much depends on the genre and nationality of the music, but it generally doesn't need to be hidden as if it's something so vulgar that it shouldn't be heard in public. Part of the artistry of interpretation lies in making breathing and phrasing as one – not in playing as many notes as possible in one breath. Circular breathing in particular is not only unnecessary but also unmusical. In some dance music, such as minuets, you can breathe squarely on the bar line to match the symmetry of dance steps and phrases.

Expressive breathing can't be schematic, mechanical or constantly predictable, unless that is the expression of a particular piece. To discover the potential of varied breathing and phrasing in identical phrases, it's worth taking the time to play strophic songs (songs in several verses to the same music), breathing and phrasing according to the words. If you try to articulate the words the way they are pronounced, it will also help you to develop variety in your articulation.

Vibrato

Most of the evidence up to and including the nineteenth century clearly states that vibrato was used purely for expressive effect, and not as an integral part of tone production. It was applied by woodwind rather than brass players, and normally done with the fingers rather than the breath. The fluctuations of finger vibrato (*flattement*) were produced by closing and opening a hole that would have only a subtle effect on the pitch. The instrument could also be shaken or rolled. The use of breath vibrato was limited to one special effect: a slow repetition of a series of notes on the same pitch and marked with dots and a slur. Modern-instrument technology and techniques nearly always require some vibrato; you need to adopt an undogmatic but thoughtful approach to it. Match your technique to the characteristics of your own instrument. Work on developing both a soft-edged and a light, bright but expressive sonority without vibrato, and learn to exercise more control over the amplitude and speed of the vibrato you already use.

Long notes were often played crescendo for half their length, then diminuendo, with vibrato added in the middle of the note. However, use this technique only if it serves the expression of the music; otherwise, like any 'style', it just becomes an irritating mannerism.

Develop an awareness, through listening, that legato passages, long sustained notes and very short notes can *gain* in expressivity when played with little or no obvious vibrato, providing there is still colour and vitality in your sound.

Ornamentation

The question to ask about any ornament is: what musical purpose does it serve? If you can understand the musical function of an ornament, it is usually a short step to making it work. While the primary purpose of all ornaments was expressive, not just to show how well you could waggle your fingers, the 'superior' technology of modern instruments can make them feel and sound clumsy. As in all aspects of performance practice, you need to extend both your mind and your technique in order to develop your playing.

There were many variations of basic ornament patterns which could be played simply and in combination. Ask yourself about the purpose and direction of ornaments. How does this ornament enhance the expression?

Fig. 5.5. Recorder player from Peter Prelleur, *The Modern Musick-Master, or The Universal Musician* (1731).

What does it do? Is it rhythmic, creating bounce and vigour? Is it melodic, helping the melody to flow? Does it move the music forward or does it suspend movement? Cadential trills can possess the feeling of both suspension and resolution. Depending on the expressive function arising from different contexts, the same ornament will need to be played with different dynamic shape, weight, length, intensity, speed, direction, beginning and resolution. Once you know how you want an ornament to sound, you can then go about shaping your technique to make that sound.

Baroque woodwind players used to practise both the technique and the invention of ornamentation; they didn't expect their ability to develop like magic. An essential technique to acquire is to learn to balance your ornaments, i.e. give them a beginning, middle and end. As an example of how to develop your abilities we will look at two principal ornaments: the trill and the appoggiatura.

Trills can be played in many different ways, including melodic, tender and quite slow, or rhythmic, brilliant and very fast. No matter whether your fingers are fast or slow, trills can always cause problems. It isn't necessarily the fastest fingers that have the easiest time; it's a matter of the control acquired from balance. To control the balance of a trill you should know: firstly, how many times you're going to beat (move your fingers up and down); and secondly, whether the pivot or balance point, highlighted by a very slight accent, lies at the start, middle or end within a given number of beats – for example, short quick trills and mordents generally balance on the first note.

To practise finding the balance point of a trill of any length, vary the number of finger movements or beats. Start with a three-beat trill on any note, say A, and *beginning with the upper note*, i.e. B–A–B–A–B–A, you will find the point of balance either at the very beginning (**B**–A–B–A–B–A) or on the third beat (B–A–B–A–**B**–A). Then practise a four-beat trill starting with the upper note – its balance point is also on the first or third beat. Follow this with five- and six-beat trills which both balance around the fifth repetition, and so on. Then include turns at the end of the trills and vary the length of the beginning upper-note appoggiaturas, from very short to very long. Practising methodically, keep to a consistent number of finger beats. Know the balance points, move your fingers freely without forcing or over-controlling them, and experiment with dynamic shape, varying the tone-colour. Constantly keep in mind the musical context of ornaments.

Appoggiaturas can be either harmonic or melodic ornaments, or both. The Italian word *appoggiare* means 'to lean', and that is exactly what appoggiaturas should do: lean (crescendo) against the harmony and towards the melody note, creating a feeling of tension. So appoggiaturas should generally start softly, crescendo, 'leaning' towards the resolution, but then making a diminuendo just before and on to the main note. There are two very effective ways of practising this technique. Firstly, keep playing the melody note *without* the appoggiatura, and don't play the appoggiatura until you understand its expression. And secondly sing – yes, sing! – the appoggiatura simultaneously with its resolution. This will help you to feel the tension that it creates and the shape arising out of that tension.

Conclusion

To discover more about how period instruments were different to play, what they did well, what sort of sound qualities they had, and how they were used in solos, ensembles and orchestras, there are several things you can do. You can listen to first-rate concert performances whenever possible; recordings can give a very distorted impression. You can try copies of period instruments out for yourself, but keep in mind that the instruments may not be the best example, and that your modern playing technique will not produce the best results. And you can look at original instruments in museum collections. But don't rely on those modern books or tutors which simply recycle misleading information, often passed around uncritically since the nineteenth century.

Keep an open mind while developing your understanding of your own instrument as it is now and as it was in the Baroque period. The best way to resolve musical and technical problems is to find out what the notes really mean. Baroque music works on the elaboration of simple ideas. A well-composed piece should be reducible to a chorale melody, i.e. conjunct melodic lines, tonic–dominant harmonies and equal rhythms. It is these underlying ideas which give the elaborated music its meaning, and the way to understanding is to strip away the elaboration and make a playable musical skeleton of the score. If you follow these basic guidelines carefully, balancing a little theory with a lot of good practice, you will undoubtedly get far more out of early music than you might have expected.

John Potter

Singing

Approaching the text

Have a look at the examples on the following pages from Handel's *Messiah*. The first (Ex. 6.1) is in the composer's own handwriting, the second (Ex. 6.2) from the Prout edition of 1902 and the third (Ex. 6.3) from Watkins Shaw's edition of 1959 (still in current use). Each one tells us a huge amount about how people of the time felt about the music, and each one gives us a different set of information about performance practice. The notes are basically the same (or are they?), but each of the twentieth-century editions adds something to Handel's original. Handel writes only a bass line for the keyboard to play, and expects the player to add the appropriate harmonies. Prout gives a metronome mark and doubles the bass line at the octave; Watkins Shaw adds extra notes and pedalling instructions; both add slurs and phrase marks. Confused? Why on earth did the composer not leave us proper instructions on how to perform his piece? It's almost as though he sketched a few ideas for the piece and left the performers to fill in the rest. In essence, this is exactly what Handel did.

The modern idea that performers and composers are separate species would have seemed very strange to Handel. He was himself one of the most brilliant keyboard players of his age, and for him, as for his fellow musicians, composing and performing were just different branches of the same musical tree. Singing instruction manuals also stress how important it is for singers to understand compositional principles too. At school, even before he began his musical studies, Handel would have learnt the art of rhetoric. Today we use this term in connection with the way an actor recites his lines on stage. In the eighteenth century and earlier, rhetoric was far more than this; it was an essential skill for everyone in public life, whether a lawyer, a politician, a singer or simply a conversationalist. Rhetoric enabled public speakers and singers to know instinctively how a text should be said or sung in the most persuasive way. This is the main reason why Handel's manuscript has no dynamic markings in the vocal part: it's not that the singer would have sung it without expression; completely the opposite, in fact. Knowledge of rhetoric would have ensured the maximum expression necessary to communicate the text.

And who was the countertenor who gave the first performance of this great alto solo? Well, it wasn't a countertenor, actually, but Susanna Cibber, who was not a singer at all (she was described as having 'a mere thread of a voice'), but was perhaps the most charismatic actress of her generation. How extraordinary that one of the second millennium's finest pieces of music was written by a composer who left most of the performing

Ex. 6.1. G. F. Handel, *Messiah*, 1741, autograph score: 'He was despised', pp. 1–2.

decisions to the performers, at least one of whom apparently couldn't really sing.

But let's assume Mrs Cibber knew a bit about singing, and try to imagine what her sound, technique and style might have been like. After all, if they were good enough for Handel, they ought to be good enough for us. *Messiah* was composed in 1741, so we need to look for a singing manual from about that date – preferably one of Italian origin, since Handel spent much of his career writing Italian operas. In 1723 a treatise on singing was published in Italy by the famous castrato Pier Francesco Tosi. An English translation appeared in 1742, and a German edition in 1757, so clearly this little book was rated pretty highly by singers of the time.

What does it tell us? Surprisingly little. For example, you won't find anything about diaphragmatic breathing, that indispensable technique that singers are all taught today. What he talks most about is the custom of ornamenting songs and arias, which confirms that Handel expected singers to choose not only their own tempo and dynamics but also quite a lot of the notes. Tosi talks of tasteful runs and trills, and about 'stealing time'. This is what we would call 'rubato', expressive slowing down and

Fig. 6.1. Mrs Susanna Cibber, engraved by John Faber, 1746, after Thomas Hudson (1701–79).

Ex. 6.2. G. F. Handel, *Messiah*, ed. Ebenezer
Prout (1902): 'He was despised', bb. 1–21.

Ex. 6.3. G. F. Handel, *Messiah*, ed. Watkins Shaw (1959): 'He was despised', bb. 1–21.

speeding up in order to complete an ornament successfully, or to put over something particularly important in the text. He lists more than twenty rules for tastefully adding your own 'passages or graces' to other people's music. The trill, or 'shake', gets a chapter to itself, and can be of many varieties, as Ex. 6.4 shows.

Ex. 6.4. J. E. Galliard, *Observations on the Florid Song* (1742), translated from P. F. Tosi, *Opinioni de' cantori antichi e moderni* (1723): types of trill.

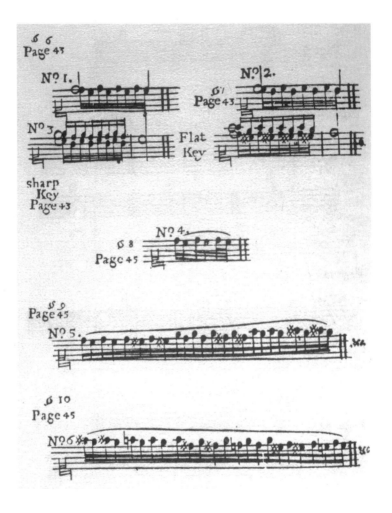

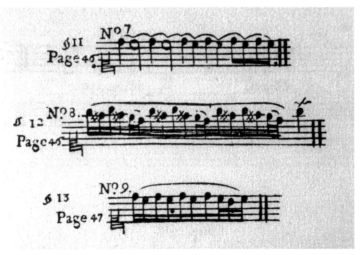

Tosi also talks at length about adding 'divisions', or 'dragging', which involves filling in the gaps between intervals (Ex. 6.5). The first line here is one that he approves of; the second he doesn't like ('Bad'!), perhaps because it was a little old-fashioned.

Ex. 6.5. Extended ornaments from Tosi.

This raises an important point: ornaments that Tosi disapproved of were clearly sufficiently widespread for him to want to criticize them. Should we be doing what Tosi wanted, or what many singers actually did? It's a matter of taste (just as it was then), and you should follow your own instincts. Some ornaments could be quite elaborate; the following examples of final cadences would have consisted of only two or three notes in the original:

Ex. 6.6. Cadential ornaments from Tosi.

Singing Baroque music

The picture that emerges from reading Tosi is of singers with light and agile voices, able to insert tasteful additions of their own into the composer's score, and capable of varying these ornaments from performance to performance. They apparently didn't have much in the way of breathing technique, and they didn't spend a lot of time trying to make a beautiful sound, being mostly concerned with delivering the text and demonstrating their virtuosity and taste. Most of what Tosi says is backed up by the German flautist Quantz, who says in his 1752 *Versuch einer Anweisung die Flöte traversiere zu spielen* (translated as *On Playing the Flute*) that ornaments must be your own, not copied from someone else, that you must be careful not to change the vowel in mid-phrase, and that there should be a seamless transition from the chest register to the head voice.

Mrs Cibber and other actresses of the time (such as Nancy Storace, who was the first Susanna in Mozart's *Le nozze di Figaro*, The Marriage of Figaro) were able to sing on an equal footing with these virtuosos because the sound of both actors and singers was probably not very different from their speech. And they didn't have to project over large orchestras into huge concert halls. This actually makes singing Baroque music particularly appropriate for young singers. One of the reasons we can make this assumption about sound is that there are no exercises in Tosi concerned with tone-colour (and there aren't any in any singing treatise before the nineteenth century). It simply wasn't an issue, as singers were prized for their own individual sound (remember there were no CDs or radio, so no one had much of a chance to copy anyone else). Although particular basses and soprano and alto castratos are often singled out, there was much less rigid categorization of voice types than we have today: singers were often described simply as singers, and it was customary to transpose music to make it comfortable to sing. Handel did have countertenors, incidentally, but these were much less common then than they are now. The countertenor today is really a modern phenomenon, and the voice has evolved to the point where countertenors take operatic roles designed for castratos. In fact, it would often be just as appropriate for women to take such roles (in that neither is historically 'correct'). There is more evidence for the French *haute-contre*, a light high tenor (and the kind of voice that would also be appropriate for Purcell's 'countertenor' lines).

There is another clue to support the idea that singers sounded more speech-like, for which we have to look a hundred years or so into Handel's future. In 1854 Manuel García, a noted singing teacher and scientist, perfected his laryngoscope, the device that specialists still use to look down your throat. García's writings confirm that in the first half of the nineteenth century there was a fundamental change in singing technique as singers started to lower their larynxes. They had new dramatic music to sing, more efficient accompanying instruments supporting them, and bigger concert halls to fill. Lowering the larynx creates more acoustic space in the vocal tract (the chamber between the cords and the lips), and means that singers can make the richer sound we associate with the modern voice, and carry over big orchestras with no extra effort. Before García there is no evidence of this technique, so we can guess that before the nineteenth century larynxes stayed fairly high, roughly where they are during normal speech. The higher position also makes the voice much more agile, because fewer muscles are tied up with tone production.

You can try this for yourself: hum a quick scale (or one of the examples from Tosi above) fairly softly and lightly, and gradually open your mouth, adding some words and articulating the fast notes in your throat. You are really speaking in song, and you don't even need vast reserves of breath to zip up and down scales. You may find at first that you articulate with a breathy 'h' sound between notes. Don't worry too much about this: a lot of singers did it, and were often criticized for it, but with practice you can minimize the 'h' and get a smooth, clear articulation. Now try to enrich the tone and project it as though you are in a big hall. It's much harder to get round the notes, you have to bring your diaphragm into play, and the sound you make becomes very different from your speaking voice. What you have done is to make the change from a pre-nineteenth-century singing voice to a modern one. This lightness of tone is characteristic of almost all Renaissance and Baroque vocal music. Madrigals, for example, would have been sung with one voice to a part, and even larger choirs would have sounded quite clear and light compared with their nineteenth-century successors.

Of course, the further back we look, the less certain the evidence becomes. A voice isn't like an instrument which you can reconstruct from a plan or a picture. The titles of earlier treatises give us clues about what was important to singers. In 1677 Pietro Reggio published a book which showed 'How to apply the best graces, with a collection of cadences plain, and then graced'. This was an ornamentation handbook for the pre-Tosi generation. Earlier still, in 1609, we find a book with the interesting title *Andreas Ornithoparcus his Micrologus*. This is a translation by the lute-song writer John Dowland of a much older treatise, published in 1517, by a German writer who took the Greek name Ornithoparchus (he was probably called something like Vogelsang, meaning 'birdsong'). It seems a bit odd that Dowland should choose to translate a book that was nearly a hundred years old, much of which is about outdated compositional methods and philosophy which he probably wouldn't have agreed with. I suspect the reason is to be found in the subtitle, *Introduction: Containing the Art of Singing*. I'm sure Dowland found Ornithoparchus's advice to singers every bit as relevant in his own day. The author makes the point that national styles are different, and he's rather embarrassed about his fellow countrymen:

> the English do carol; the French sing, the Spaniards weep, the Italians... caper with their voices; the others bark, but the Germans (which I am ashamed to utter) do howl like wolves...

(A bit hard on the Germans, I think.)

Ornithoparchus sets out ten basic rules for singers. These include making the most of the words, not changing the vowel in mid-phrase (as Tosi and Quantz would say over 200 years later), not singing too loud (no 'braying like an ass') and not opening the mouth too wide ('a sign of a mad singer'). Beneath the humour, there is a serious point about national styles: if your singing is related to your speech, then if you are French or Italian your singing will take on the characteristics of those languages. You have to find what actors' dialect coaches call the 'vocal set' for each language you sing in. An easy way to do this is to speak your own language but with the accent of the language you wish to sing, then change to the foreign language while consciously keeping your voice in the same place. It is also worth noting that until quite late in the nineteenth century there was no standard English accent (and a similar situation prevailed in most other countries during the Baroque period and earlier). This means not only that the singers were making the words clear, but that they would be using the geographical accent of their everyday speech.

There was, of course, more to it than simply singing. Those capering Italians were also observed by the music theorist Marin Mersenne in 1636 in a fascinating glimpse of their recitative singing. He says:

they represent as much as they can the passions and affections of the soul and spirit, as for example anger, furore, disdain, rage, the frailties of the heart, and many other passions, with a violence so strange that one would almost say that they are touched by the same emotions they are representing in the song...

You can almost see and hear them doing it, and their recitative must have been very dramatic indeed, confirming the rhetorical nature of singing during this period. Songs were performed not just with the voice, but using every possible means to make the text more expressive. Similarly exciting singing had been heard by Vincenzo Giustiniani, the Roman nobleman who in 1628 wrote an account of the singing he had witnessed at the court of Ferrara during the 1570s, where the singers

moderated or increased their voices, loud or soft, heavy or light...now slow, breaking off with sometimes a gentle sigh, now singing long passages legato or detached, now groups, now leaps, now with long trills, now with short, and again with sweet running passages sung softly... They made the words clear in such a way that one could hear even the last syllable of every word...

And it looked good, too:

They accompanied the music and the sentiment with appropriate facial expressions, glances and gestures, with no awkward movements of the mouth or hands or body which might not express the feeling of the song.

The composer and singing teacher Emilio de' Cavalieri (1600) also says that a singer should be as expressive as possible:

and in particular he should express the words well, so that they may be understood, and accompany them with gestures and movements, not only of the hands but other gestures that are efficacious aids in moving the affections.

This insistence on the importance of the words was made clear by Giulio Cesare Monteverdi, in his preface to his brother Claudio's fifth book of madrigals (1605), when he famously said that the music 'becomes the servant of the words, and the words the mistress of the harmony'.

Conclusion

In our search backwards from the late Baroque, we are beginning to see that the same problems had been worrying composers and performers for perhaps hundreds of years, and we can begin to form a picture of what singing might have been like at any given time during our period. Here's a provisional list of what has emerged so far:

- The sound was very individual, related to the singers' speech.
- The words are of equal importance to the music.
- Anything which aids expressivity can be incorporated into the performance.
- Singers were expected to have a knowledge of ornamentation (and good taste!).

- Tempos could be flexible.
- Voices were small, light and nimble.

Two topics that singers always worry about are tuning and vibrato. The kind of tuning you use depends on what instruments (if any) you have accompanying you. If you are singing with a piano, there are no alterations that you can make: the piano is tuned in equal temperament so that all keys sound the same. If you are singing with old instruments or *a cappella* then you can try 'just intonation'. This is a way of relating your tuning to the harmonic series (the overtones contained within each note; see Ex. 5.1, p. 89). Relative to the piano, this means keeping major 3rds very slightly lower, and minor 3rds a little higher. You will also find yourself singing slightly wider 5ths and slightly narrower 4ths. Major and minor 2nds should be wider, but chromatic semitones smaller; accidental flats should be thought higher, and sharps lower. But don't forget that tuning is simply a means to an end, it's not something singing treatises spend a long time discussing: passion was more important. As for pitch, if the piece was not in a comfortable key, singers had no hesitation in transposing it.

Vibrato should also not be a source of worry. Baroque sources rarely mention it, and it is really only from the nineteenth century onwards that it becomes an issue. It clearly didn't worry pre-Romantic musicians whether they used vibrato or not. There are two things you need to bear in mind, though: tuning in ensembles is much easier if you reduce the vibrato; and vibrato is something that doesn't occur in speech. Since the sources often say that singing should be speech-like, we might gather from this they would not have used much vibrato. In the end, it's up to you and the natural sound you make.

We can now begin to see how Handel could have preferred Mrs Cibber as his alto soloist in *Messiah*. The celebrated historian Charles Burney says that her 'voice and manners softened his severity for her want of musical knowledge'. As an actress she would have lived by her speaking voice and been very used to moving listeners by her rhetorical delivery, doing what-ever was necessary to put over the text (which for Handel was every bit as important as his own music).

Returning to 'He was despised', we can see how a historically informed approach might work. Let's start with the tempo. 'Largo' is Handel's orig-inal mark and we have no way of knowing what he meant by this. Slow, certainly, but relative to what? The phrases are mostly short, and we can assume that Mrs Cibber did not possess anything like a modern breathing technique, so it can't be too slow. She would have sung the punctuation, breaking at commas for rhetorical effect. She would have breathed, possibly audibly and dramatically between phrases, with very little sense of musical line as we now understand it. She would have accented the phrases as in speech. A lot of her phrases are accompanied only by the keyboard, and she would have been very free with the tempo at these points, going for maximum pathos and expressivity. Her voice was small, so the playing would have been light and the phrasing would have matched her speech rhythm, with small accelerandos and slowings (taking time, as the sources tell us so often).

Prout adds extra notes to the accompaniment without saying which are his and which are Handel's. Watkins Shaw makes additions to the vocal part in small notes to distinguish them from what Handel actually wrote. These are the kinds of ornament that Mrs Cibber might have done. We know from our brief survey of the sources that it was important for singers to invent their own, so these should be thought of only as examples. It would be as inappropriate to reproduce these unaltered as it would be to sing the aria with no ornamentation at all. You can easily find for yourself similar ways of filling in decorative bits between the composer's own notes (and helpful clues will also be found in other chapters of this book). You will have noticed that there are no expression marks in the voice part. Ironically, this is the most telling aspect of the score. You are free to be as expressive as you like with whatever means you have at your disposal. That's what Handel wanted, and it's certainly what he got from Susanna Cibber.

Clifford Bartlett

Sources and Editions

What does notation mean?

Language is expressed in words, which can be written down. What you are reading now would mean the same if you were to hear me speak it. Some words require performance to have their full effect. 'To be or not to be' or Martin Luther King's 'I have a dream...' have meaning on the printed page, but need to be heard for their emotional significance to have their full effect: those who have not heard a recording of Martin Luther King delivering his speech would find it very difficult to imagine how it sounded from the printed text. The problem with musical notation is that the information it gives is limited: it gives the bare text, but has to be interpreted by the performer to become music.

The amount of information that the notation needs to give has varied over the centuries, in most respects becoming more precise. But at different times there have been different priorities for what it was most important to convey. The early notation of plainchant is vague with regard to pitch but subtly detailed with regard to the shaping of the phrases. When precise indication of the pitch became normal, other subtleties were lost. This may be seen in the *Graduale triplex* (Solesmes, 1979), an edition of the plainchant for the Mass in which the late-medieval notation (which remained normal in Roman Catholic service books until the 1970s) is accompanied by the signs from two manuscripts from the tenth century. When two or more parts are performed together, rhythmic precision becomes more important, and by the fourteenth century a complex system existed for showing note-lengths. This was simplified into the modern system in the seventeenth century; it is still a matter of debate how long the earlier rules for relating duple and triple time were remembered.

In the Baroque period the chief function of written music was to show the notes and rhythms. Later, when composers paid far more attention to indicating dynamics, phrasing and other nuances, it was thought necessary to update the notation of older music by adding signs to make music of the past look like modern music. This was related to matters of performance practice, since it was expected that old music would be played like music of the present, on the same instruments and in the same style. Such editions were normal until quite recently. So if an elderly relative offers you a pile of music, be duly grateful but be extremely cautious in using it. (This is not, incidentally, just a problem with early music; editions of nineteenth-century repertoire are just as likely to be outmoded.)

Whenever I have attended a masterclass, one of the most common pieces of advice given by all sorts of famous performers has been: study what the composer wrote. Sometimes they recommend looking at the autograph score, although that is not always the sole authority. Anyone who is studying a piece of music should be quite sure that the information on the page is as reliable as possible. If you are seriously practising a piece of music, every detail is significant. But if the authority of the detail is questionable, you are in a false position. However eminent the names associated with added performance suggestions, what they suggest can only be one possible interpretation: what may have worked well for them may not work for you. Moreover, we are now more sympathetic to and know more about Baroque performance practice than musicians of the older generation.

Looking at editions

What is there in older editions that should raise our suspicions? Ex. 7.1 shows the opening of the last movement of Sonata No. 6 from the Op. 2 of Pietro Antonio Locatelli, as published by Augener in 1920. The title page reads *Sonata da camera for violin & piano. F. David's edition. Edited and Revised by Emile Sauret*. (Ferdinand David, 1810–73, was a great violinist and teacher, and gave the first performance of Mendelssohn's Concerto. Sauret, 1852–1920, was also a virtuoso violinist and teacher, and had periods teaching at the Royal Academy of Music and Trinity College of Music in London.) At first, try not to look at the original reproduced as Ex. 7.2 on page 110: one does not always have access to a better edition for comparison. What is there in Ex. 7.1 that we should disbelieve?

Dynamics

In music of this period (the sonata was first published in 1732, information that the edition does not include), louds and softs are very rarely notated; when they appear, they usually indicate a simple echo. 'Hairpins' for crescendo and diminuendo did not come into use until a little later. A violinist may quite possibly have treated the opening bar as an introductory phrase, with a crescendo leading up to a firm g''; similarly the next phrase, marked p by the editor, may be played more softly. But the frequency of the *f*s and *p*s is entirely uncharacteristic of the notation of the period: their presence exaggerates the dynamic range that is appropriate, and discourages the performer from finding a suitable pattern of more gentle rises and falls.

Slurs

Added slurs can be more difficult to detect, since there may well have been some in the original edition. Except in embellishments in slower movements, original slurs tend to be short (over two or three notes) and within a beat rather than crossing from one beat to the next. So it is likely that none of the slurs is original. (Editions of this type often include long phrase-marks running across several bars; these are characteristic of nineteenth-century music but were not used in the Baroque period.)

Accompaniment

At this period a solo sonata will have been accompanied by continuo: visually, that is, a single bass-line, which can be played (depending on

Ex. 7.1.
P. A. Locatelli,
Sonata in G minor
Op. 2 No. 6, ed. Emile
Sauret, Augener
Edition (1920): fourth
movement, bb. 1–11.

circumstances) by keyboard or plucked string instrument and/or a melodic bass instrument (see Chapter 3 'Keyboard', pp. 57–9 and Chapter 4 'Strings', pp. 81–2). This version is obviously not intended for the most common keyboard instrument of Locatelli's time, the harpsichord: one would not expect that in the 1920s. But even on the piano it would seem reasonable to base a performance on dynamics that made some sense in relation to when the piece was written. A good harpsichordist will vary the dynamics by the thickness of chords and by articulation; there is no way that the markings here can be reproduced on the instrument. It is also unlikely that the player will want to double the bass line with octaves as here. But which is the proper octave to play? At first it seems to be the upper one, but at bar 3 the upper octave stops, so one would presume that the lower octave is the original.

We can now turn the page to see what the original edition looks like (Ex. 7.2).

Ex. 7.2.
P. A. Locatelli,
Sonata in G minor
Op. 2 No. 6, original
edition (1732): fourth
movement, bb. 1–13.

The first surprise is that the editor has invented the opening: he must have thought that a movement that sounded like a song needed a lead-in. The octave register of the bass was indeed confusing, and in fact our guess was wrong for bar 1 (= bar 3). We were also right to suspect the slurring: it is far more characteristic of late-Baroque style to emphasize the first note of the bar. There are no dynamics.

There are other features of the original edition that are different in the 1920 edition. The tempo marking has been changed. One expects the last movement of a sonata to be quick, especially if it is notated in the gigue tempo of 12/8. Locatelli uses that signature only for the upper part: the accompaniment is in **c** (i.e. 4/4 time). This is a notation of convenience. It is much easier to write and read the bass part with four crotchets to a bar than with four dotted crotchets, though it is played as if in 12/8. (It is very common, though not universal, that triplets and ♪.♪ should be played identically. See Chapter 2 'Notation and Interpretation, pp. 39–40.) The extra rests in Sauret's accompaniment are a useful reminder that the notation tells you when a note starts, not how long it is sustained; the composer leaves the decision to the performer (though not to an editor). Sauret's modernization of the key signature causes no problems here; but more on that topic later.

It will be seen that Sauret takes some of the melody notes down an octave. It is not entirely clear why he has done this, but an explanation may lie in the title of the original publication: *XII sonate à flauto traversiere solo è basso*. (So this isn't a violin sonata at all!) Sauret evidently thought that Locatelli changed the expected shape of the phrase because the lower notes would have sounded weak on the flute, whereas on the violin they were no problem.

There is one further problem with the 1920 edition. Editors sometimes add suggestions to the solo part that are not included in the solo line as printed in the score. It will be seen from Ex. 7.3 that the bowings and dynamics are as in the score, but that bow-directions and fingerings have been added. This practice has by no means died out, and it is confusing in that the accompanist, who may well be the more experienced musician, does not have before him or her what the soloist is reading, so needs continually to stand up and look at the part in order to offer any help; and the soloist has even more additional clutter separating his or her music from the original.

Ex. 7.3.
P. A. Locatelli, Sonata in G minor Op. 2 No. 6, ed. Emile Sauret: fourth movement, solo part, bb. 1–11.

I have taken a fairly extreme example: but editions of this nature are still in print, especially from firms specializing in reprints rather than those commissioning new editions. We have learnt from it some of the signs by which a bad edition can be detected.

The reason why many musicians find music of the Baroque period so rewarding is that so much is left to the performer. The allocation of responsibilities between composer and performer was different, and the former was not expected to exercise as much control over the latter as in later periods. Often, of course, the composer was directly involved in the performance of his music; but there is little sign that, when composers prepared editions of their music, they felt obliged to add anything to the notation to make up for the lack of their personal input when the editions were performed.

You can, of course, only take advantage of this if you have achieved some understanding of how to do this within the constraints appropriate to the style. Once you have done so, you will realize why editions that tell you what to do are so constricting and so against the ethos of early music.

Finding a good edition

The performer needs to relate directly to what the composer wrote and establish an individual interpretation from that, within the stylistic guidelines suggested in earlier chapters of this book. Getting a 'clean' edition is one step. Some such editions are described as 'Urtext'. (That is a German word meaning roughly 'original text'.) In the second half of the nineteenth century, the complete works of many of the great composers – Palestrina, Lassus, Schütz, Corelli, Bach, Handel, Mozart, Beethoven, Schubert, Mendelssohn, Schumann – were published in editions without additional performing suggestions. In the last fifty years, publishers such as Lea Pocket Scores, Edwin Kalmus and Dover Books have produced reprints from these, offering students cheap Urtext editions. These are extremely useful, but there is no guarantee that the musical texts they contain are accurate in more than the negative sense that they do not contain editorial additions.

'Edit' has two meanings. One is for the process applied by Sauret to Locatelli: taking the music and showing how the editor thinks it should be played. (You will find the word 'revised' on older editions, but it has now fallen out of use.) It is still, in a more restrained and responsible form, a legitimate process in providing material for students at early stages of their instruction. But the other meaning is to establish the musical text: to decide what notes and ancillary information should be printed in an Urtext edition.

The 'sources' of an edition are the original documents upon which the edition is based. If we are lucky, this will include the composer's autograph. But even if this exists, it is not necessarily authoritative: it may not present the final state of a work; indeed, there may not be a final version. We are lucky that Handel kept virtually all his manuscripts together, and they now survive in The British Library. They are invaluable documents for studying a composer at work, and it is easy from them to imagine him writing at high speed (he normally wrote an opera or oratorio in less than a month), taking as many short cuts as possible (for a Handel autograph score, see Ex. 6.1, pp. 96–7). His autograph manuscript was not convenient for use at performance, so a neater score was prepared by a copyist. It was this that Handel used subsequently. So changes were marked in the copyist's score, not the autograph. And changes there usually were. Even before the first performance, there may have been changes of cast involving alterations in the music. When a work was revived later, the singers were usually different, so more changes were needed. Every year in which Handel performed *Messiah* there were differences. There is no authoritative version. All the editor can do is consult the sources and present the user with all the options. (Many editions, going right back to the eighteenth century, have included alternative settings.)

A score does not necessarily tell us exactly what was played; but individual parts sometimes can, especially as most major works were written for performances at which the composer was present. We are lucky that the parts used for the original performances of some of Bach's cantatas survive. These are mostly written by copyists, but often have additions by the composer, giving performance indications that do not appear on the autographs. Musicologists tend to be more accustomed to working with scores, so only recently has the information available from the parts always been taken seriously. (Compare, for instance, the first movement of Bach's Mass in B minor in the Bärenreiter edition of 1956, based on the score, and the Peters edition of 1997, which includes many more slurs from the parts.) Sets of orchestral parts are also useful because they sometimes include instruments not mentioned in the score. The autograph of *Messiah* has no mention of oboes or bassoons, but when the opening *Sinfony* was published in 1743, oboe parts were included; and the only complete set of performing parts, copied for the Foundling Hospital in London according to the terms of Handel's will, includes oboes and bassoons.

There is a further source of information for vocal music: libretti (separate publication of the words). Bach's congregation and Handel's opera and oratorio audience had the words available to read during the performance. Sometimes the printed texts agree with the musical sources, sometimes they differ. The composer was not usually concerned with accurate orthography or punctuation. Editors sometimes normalize the composer's words according to modern publishing rules, but an alternative is to follow the practice of the contemporary printer. However, if the composer makes a change of any significance, his version should be followed.

A simple check on whether an edition is likely to respect the composer's intent is whether it states the sources on which it is based. Even if the introduction or critical commentary is in a language that you do not understand, the presence of this information is usually obvious. You can also look for such telltale signs as any accidentals, dynamics or other matter in square brackets, indicating an addition by the editor. Some editions use variation in typeface to distinguish original and editorial matter: Bärenreiter, for instance, uses roman for original text, italic for editorial. This can be confusing, since most other publishers use italic font for the original tempos and dynamics and put editorial ones in square brackets.

When a modern composer or editor submits a manuscript (or computer-set score) to a publisher, a copy-editor is appointed to read it in meticulous detail. He or she will look out for misprints, but beyond that will point out inconsistencies, places that seem not to make sense, and other features that seem questionable. Even if there is only one source, the editor of an early work has to give it this treatment, but without recourse to the composer to confirm his or her hunches! Some mistakes are obvious, and must have been obvious at the time. But we should not be too surprised that they were not corrected; the cheap graphite pencil was not yet invented, crayons were clumsy, and an ink-pot and quill pen were hardly convenient to use at rehearsal. (So don't believe the idea that performances must have been terrible because there are uncorrected mistakes in original parts: people had better memories then.) But it is not always clear whether a note that looks odd is wrong or a stroke of imagination.

An editor is expected to compare the sources, discuss the relationship between them, list significant differences, and show how his or her edition changes the notation from that of the major source. Some modernizations are acceptable, indeed are expected, provided that they are stated; but these are diminishing as performers get more used to using reproductions of original Baroque publications or manuscripts, known as facsimiles. There are both musical and financial reasons for their use.

Until about twenty-five years ago, facsimiles were expensive objects that only large libraries could afford, and which were allowed to be used only within their walls: they were assumed to be for study, not for performance. It was lutenists who began to change that. They can play from the original notation far more easily than from transcriptions, because of the way lute music is written in tablature. (In tablature, the notation tells you not what note you should be playing, but where and when to put your fingers on the strings.) There were not enough lutenists for transcriptions to be economically viable, but there were facsimiles of the original notation which could be played from. Gradually prices came down, as more players of other instruments and singers realized that there were positive advantages in using facsimiles and that the difficulties, especially for music of the eighteenth century, were not great. So now there is an economic advantage as well as a musical one, in that it is possible to buy a set of six sonatas in their original form as cheaply as it would cost to buy one in a modern edition.

Not all music of the period is available and performable from facsimile. Printed editions are usually more legible than manuscript, although not all music was printed. The prevalence of printing differed across Europe. Amsterdam, London and Paris were the centres of the publishing industry, and editions were produced in these cities of music by most composers of note. Music produced elsewhere was often less legible: Telemann, for instance, issued a large number of his own publications in Hamburg, but only the quartets published in Paris are easy on the eye. Bach, too, suffered from local production; there were no internationally circulated editions of his music until the nineteenth century, and they have no particular authority.

In the seventeenth century there had been much more music printing in Italy, especially Venice, but with different technology. The best eighteenth-century editions were engraved, the method that remained in use until quite recently. Previously, printed music was set from individual bits of metal (Ex. 7.4) like the letters used for printing books. The stave lines were made up of a series of individual bits, which often did not meet exactly, and each note was separate, so there could be no beaming (lines joining the tops or bottoms of the stems). It is thus very difficult to see the pattern in long passages of quavers or semiquavers, so playing fluently from such editions is quite difficult. It is best to avoid them until you are a confident reader of later facsimiles.

Facsimiles of manuscripts are often primarily intended for scholars; they are usually of scores rather than parts, and are often difficult to read. It is a pity that so few parts of Bach's instrumental music have been published in facsimile, but one reason is the poor survival rate – most of the surviving performing sets are of church music. Frustratingly, one major source that has been issued in facsimile, the Kyrie and Gloria of the Mass in B minor, was out of print at the time of writing.

It should be remembered that early printed editions are not always entirely reliable. In the case of Handel's instrumental music, for instance, they are recommended only for the trio sonatas Op. 2 and the concerti grossi Op. 6.

Ex. 7.4. G. Torelli, Concerto grosso Op. 8 No. 10, solo violin part, as printed in Bologna in 1709 using movable type. Compare this with the much clearer Ex. 7.2, which uses the more modern technique of engraving.

Notation in Baroque sources

The following paragraphs list some areas in which earlier notation differs from modern. It points out what an editor will have changed, or what you need to be prepared for if you are thinking of using facsimiles.

Clefs

Performers were accustomed to a wider range of clefs than we use now. Treble parts were sometimes written with a C or a G clef on the bottom line; viola parts might have had the C clef on any line except the top. Continuo parts often changed clefs, and used more clefs, than in modern editions. Choral parts used the soprano (C on bottom line), alto (C on middle line), tenor (C on fourth line) and bass clefs, though solo tenor parts sometimes used the modern convention of being written an octave higher in treble clef, especially in printed sources. Occasionally parts for male altos were also printed an octave higher: if there is a top C in a song from Purcell's time, it is not for a soprano.

Beaming

Eighteenth-century engraved editions and manuscripts generally use the same rules for beaming, the joining of note stems, as modern publishers. Seventeenth-century practice was different because of the printing process. Some editions are now preserving the original beaming in seventeenth-century keyboard music, to the extent of giving each note in a chord a separate tail; but perhaps those who can benefit from such details should be using facsimiles rather than modern editions. One change of convention is that modern publishers are more likely to beam instrumental and vocal music in the same way, whereas in the eighteenth century notes with separate syllables had separate beams. A disadvantage of modernization is that, if the underlay (text-setting) printed in an edition looks awkward, a singer may be tempted to change it without realizing that it is explicit in the original.

Key signatures and accidentals

The modern conventions for key signatures were gradually established through the Baroque period. In 1610 Monteverdi wrote the first movement of his Vespers in D major but with no signature. At the end of the seventeenth century, Corelli used just two sharps as a signature for A major. Throughout the period, it was normal for flat minor keys to have one flat fewer than we expect. This notation sometimes survives into modern editions. When using facsimiles, don't guess the key from the number of sharps or flats in the signature: they are often placed at both octaves.

Accidentals followed a different convention from that in use now, according to which an accidental stays in force until the next bar line. Then, an accidental applied to repetitions of the same note, but if another note intervened before a recurrence of the same pitch, then the accidental was no longer valid. Not all composers, copyists and printers followed the system with absolute logic, so common sense is needed. Until recently, editors changed the notation to the modern convention. But if there are ambiguities, it is very difficult to show what is in the source. Editors are beginning to retain the older convention, though generally inserting cautionary accidentals when an accidental ceases to apply to a note later in the bar, so that the user is aware of a greater number of accidentals than expected. The old convention has its practical merits: I was intrigued to find a copy of Bach's 'forty-eight' in which I had in my youth pencilled lots of additional accidentals to make sure I played the right notes; I later found they were all in the autograph but had been omitted by the editor as being superfluous by modern rules. The use of the natural sign increased during the Baroque period; but expect sharps to be cancelled by flats and vice versa.

Bar lines

Early in the period, parts were still printed in the older manner, without bar lines; when they do occur, they often indicate the ends of sections, and are the equivalent of double bars. By the end of the seventeenth century, regular barring was normal, though occasionally the length of bars may be doubled or halved without any change of time signature. (Time signatures only gradually changed from their earlier function of relating to the beat, not the bar.) Scores always had bar lines, though not necessarily at regular intervals. Most editors regularize the barring and may subdivide long bars. You may come across editions in which the editor has drawn attention to hemiola cadences in triple time (two bars of three combined into one bar of six) by omitting a bar line (sometimes, in fact, following the sources). But most musicians find it simpler for the barring to be regular, even if the music contradicts it.

Repeats

Precision in the notation of repeats increased during the period. Printed sources use the sign :‖: even when the music on only one side of the sign is repeated. Binary movements (in two halves) should normally have repeats, whether there are any repeat marks or not. French music in particular often has an additional repeat of the last few bars (the *petite reprise*), marked by tiny signs which can easily be missed. Early sources are much less careful in sorting out first- and second-time bars, leaving it to the good sense of the player. Most modern editors correct this.

Dynamics

Supplementation of dynamics is now applied far more cautiously than in the Locatelli example above. When people first started trying to play Baroque music in a period style, the term 'terraced dynamics' was invented. By analogy with the organ (and by false analogy with the harpsichord), it was assumed that the music went along at one steady volume, then abruptly became louder or softer. There is some encouragement for this in the markings in music for solo voice and orchestra, which often has lots of *f*s and *p*s in the orchestral parts. But those markings, although they obviously have some dynamic significance, function chiefly as cues to warn the players when they are accompanying and when they can play out. Otherwise, they are usually used to indicate echoes. But it now seems more likely that large-scale dynamic changes were less important than the shaping of the phrases, which involves gradual changes in volume. The scope for editorial dynamics is quite small.

Keyboard music

In addition to a variety of clefs, players of music from the seventeenth century may also have to negotiate staves with more than the standard five lines. The technique is to navigate by the place of the clef rather than the top or bottom of the stave. It was also common to give separate stems to each note, even when writing chords. These features are not usually preserved in modern editions, but will be encountered by those using facsimiles of Frescobaldi and his Italian contemporaries (see Ex. 3.5, p. 64). Contrapuntal keyboard music was sometimes notated in open score, the best known example being Bach's *Die Kunst der Fuge* (The Art of Fugue).

German organists had their individual form of tablature, with letters used for each contrapuntal line; as yet, modern organists are not expected to play from it. There are difficulties in imagining what earlier tablature sources might have been like when only staff-notation sources survive. Editors of organ music by Buxtehude or other north German composers of his time, working from slightly later sources that have been transcribed into staff notation, need to imagine what the original notation may have looked like before they can produce their own staff-notation editions. If your edition does not discuss this topic, find another one. Much organ music up to and including Bach was, when not in tablature, written on two staves, not three, and the sources are not always clear on what is played by the pedal.

Solo keyboard players have the advantage of not being dependent on the abilities of an accompanist in their choice of edition; but the disadvantage is that most of the repertoire is available in editions that, although in many respects properly edited, are not true Urtexts (even in series with 'Urtext' in their title) in that fingering has been added, generally with the piano in mind. There are two reasons to deplore fixing fingering in print. One is that every hand is different, so what suits one person may not suit another. The other is that you may want to experiment with fingerings of the period, and few published fingerings take that into account; indeed, modern suggestions often contradict the implied phrasing. Fortunately, it is possible to train yourself not to notice modern suggestions.

Continuo

The factor that most inhibits the use of facsimiles is the need for a keyboard player who can manage without a realization (written-out version) of the continuo. Some writers have characterized the Baroque as the era of the figured bass. The system arose around 1600 and, although it was a long time dying, its importance diminished from around 1750. The ability to play from the bass is now essential for specialist professionals, but it is not an accomplishment widely acquired by music teachers or amateur players. This is a pity. It is far less difficult than most people imagine, and requires, apart from a basic knowledge of harmony, chiefly confidence and lots of playing experience: you learn by doing it, rather than studying how to do it. It gets expensive if the soloist prefers to use a facsimile but the accompanist needs a modern edition. (For more on continuo playing see Chapter 3 'Keyboard', pp. 57–9.)

Unfortunately, there are very few realizations that are effective as they stand. Most editors now write a fairly simple version; this is useful, since you can then adapt it for the instrument you are using to suit your manner of playing. Such small-scale adaptation provides a foretaste of the freedom from notation that you will have when you eventually abandon the notated realization. Whether a realized part is used or not, you must be aware that your main functions are to play the bass and to support the soloist. In fact, it is good practice to start by playing just the bass part without adding the chords, concentrating on playing it musically; then occasionally add chords at cadences. If you have the flair and a good harmonic sense, you will find that the other chords will mostly fall into place without too much effort.

The choice of edition may well be made by the soloist, not the keyboard player. So here are a few clues as to what you should avoid, if there is any choice available:

- realizations that look like harpsichord concertos: not only are they unstylish, but also the player will be far too busy trying to get the part right to concentrate on accompanying properly;
- realizations that look thick and congested: it is far easier to add notes than leave them out;
- realizations that go too high: depending on the instrument, notes above the top of the treble stave can either stick out unpleasantly or sound thin. Baroque writers suggest that accompaniments should not go above the stave, and they were thinking of a stave with a soprano, not a treble, clef with a *d″* as the top line. Modern realizations tend to be higher than one would naturally play because of the convention of only using the upper stave, keeping the lower stave exclusively for the original bass part. This makes it easy to distinguish the original from the realization, but makes it difficult to observe one of the principles of continuo accompaniment, which is to keep the hands close together;
- in music from the earlier seventeenth century, realizations that have minor dominant and tonic chords at cadences.

Music from printed eighteenth-century sources should normally have bass figures: their absence should make you suspicious. But not all seventeenth-century music was figured, and throughout the period figuring was often added by the publisher, so editions based on manuscripts may well be unfigured. Modern publishers rarely add figures, except when the source is so thoroughly figured that it is sensible to supplement occasional omissions.

If you are lucky enough to have a lutenist as accompanist (preferably playing one of the larger members of the lute family, the theorbo or archlute), you will not need a realized edition, since lutenists who accompany Baroque music learn to play from the bass; those who can't will need to prepare their own tablature part.

Many editions of late Baroque music include a separate part for a melodic bass instrument (I'll refer to it as cello, but it might also be a viola da gamba or bassoon). It is not essential always to have a cello playing the bass as well as a keyboard (and on the other hand, some music works well with a melodic instrument but without a keyboard). In the early Baroque period, composers sometimes made a distinction: in the two sets of sonatas by Dario Castello, for instance, first published in the 1620s, some have a part for a solo bass instrument as well as for continuo, others have just a continuo part. Eighteenth-century editions of 'Solos', i.e. music for one solo instrument and continuo, were usually published as two-stave scores, and some modern editions make an attempt to reproduce this by supplying two copies of the music in this format as parts, though omitting bass figures. Trio sonatas, however, were published in parts. Sometimes there were separate copies for cello and harpsichord, but often they were expected to share. Eighteenth-century players seem to have had better sight than modern ones, since it was quite normal for a cellist to read from the copy on the harpsichord (e.g. Fig. 4.2, p. 71). In fact, this helps enormously with ensemble and phrasing. (For an instance where it didn't work, look up Michel Corrette in *The New Grove Dictionary of Music and Musicians*.)

Singers

It is singers who will find it most difficult to obtain editions with suitable accompaniments. There are a variety of editions of *arie antiche*, for instance, with keyboard parts that bear no relation to the original, and which give the harpsichordist the impossible task of playing something stylish from a piano accompaniment like that of the Locatelli example earlier in this chapter. There is the further problem that the accompaniment may have been written for orchestra (instrumental concertos with keyboard reductions present the same problem). Trying to include every note of the original orchestration can be counter-productive. It is important that the keyboard part distinguishes between orchestral reduction and continuo realization; apart from this being useful information for the player, the singer needs to know what is fixed and what is variable, in case an opportunity comes to perform with an orchestra.

Many editors have seen the apparent emptiness of texture in songs with continuo as a compositional challenge. This is particularly so with the songs of Purcell, and very few editions have proper continuo realizations. (In my view, the best is *Thirty Songs in Two Volumes* edited by Timothy Roberts, Oxford University Press, 1995.) Accompaniments of early seventeenth-century songs, too, tend to be far too elaborate, not necessarily from the invention of irrelevant countermelodies, but because the editor is not prepared to add simple chords to the bass and let passing dissonances in the vocal part clash with them.

It is essential that the singer should understand the words. It is helpful if the poem is set out as a poem, so that you have some idea of the poetic shape. You will also need to know where the lines begin, and whether any word repetition is structural, if you reach the stage of printing programmes with texts for a concert. If the text is foreign and you are not familiar with the language, you will need to find a translation, and it is helpful if it is printed alongside the original language. (Singing translations are not usually close enough to be very helpful in showing what each word means.)

The use of facsimiles presents additional problems to singers. The underlay may not be quite so carefully printed as one expects in good modern editions, though the beaming of quavers is helpful. In Italian, beware of elisions (dropping syllables or vowels to run words together): mistakes occur even in the complete edition of Monteverdi edited by Malipiero, who was an Italian! The similarity between 'f' and 's' can cause problems, especially in Italian, since there are common words where 'f' and 's' can both make sense (*fia* and *sia*, for example). In German, beware of ß (= ss). In early seventeenth-century Latin texts 'i' and 'j' are interchangable, as are 'u' and 'v', and you may still find the medieval abbreviation of a line over a vowel meaning that it is followed by an 'm' or 'n'. You may also find 'ij' in isolation, meaning 'repeat the previous set of words'. If you can manage to cope with the original notation, there is a vast repertoire of seventeenth-century Latin motets and Italian and French cantatas in facsimile in the various series Garland Publishing has produced (nearly all out of print, but libraries should let you photocopy individual items).

Much of the early vocal repertoire consists of opera arias. Most separate editions are bad, so it is usually better to check a score of the complete opera. Singers usually ask for vocal scores, but nearly all Baroque operas are scored so lightly that both singer and accompanist can work from a full score. (In fact, in the whole of Monteverdi's three operas, the solo voice is never actually accompanied by instruments other than continuo, though in a couple of arias there is close alternation.) If you need a Handel opera aria (and, if you are an alto or tenor, you are prepared to cope with the old clefs), it is best to get hold of the nineteenth-century Chrysander edition (large libraries will have the original, or the Gregg or Kalmus reprints) and photocopy what you want (no copyright is involved; with more recent editions, of course, you must be careful to observe copyright laws).

Educational editions

You may well think that I am undermining some of the editions published by the Associated Board of the Royal Schools of Music. I do, in fact, question the ubiquitous fingering. But there is a place for editions that guide the player towards the proper conventions of the music, and those of keyboard music by Bach and Handel prepared for the Associated Board by Richard Jones are models of their kind: practical information added to a musical text which is the product of meticulous scholarship, and with thorough introductions and commentaries. His four-volume anthology of Baroque violin music is similarly helpful.

Finding out more

There are many books on performance practice (some are listed in the Suggestions for Further Reading towards the end of this book). But musicians have traditionally learnt by ear, and performers of Baroque music, even if they are using modern instruments, should study the various ways in which our specialist performers interpret the bare bones of the notation. It is helpful to follow performances with a good edition. The practice of taking a score to concerts has declined as the amount of music on record has increased; but do listen to the radio and CDs with the music in front of you, and ask yourself how and why the performers have diverged from what is notated. It is also useful to go to courses. In the UK the various early music forums run courses and workshops (often directed by leading performers); some expect players to use Baroque instruments, but others are happy to accept anyone who is interested in playing in the appropriate style – though you should check what pitch is being used. There is a conventional late-Baroque pitch of $a' = 415$ Hz (a semitone below modern pitch of $a' = 440$), but music from the later eighteenth century is often played at $a' = 430$, and French music may be at $a' = 390$ (down a tone) (see also Chapter 2 'Notation and Interpretation', pp. 23–4). If you don't have a suitable instrument, it may still be worth going along to listen to what the conductor or teacher has to say. Summer schools are particularly useful, since there is often time to talk to the teachers (and perhaps have a lesson). In the UK, concerts, courses and events are listed in *Early Music News* and *Early Music Review*, the latter including some outside the UK. Other countries have similar sources, such as *Early Music America* in the USA.

How do you find good editions and facsimiles? With the rapidly expanding repertoire, few shops can hold a comprehensive stock of any sort of music. There are dealers who can often be helpful on the phone, but there is no guarantee that the right person will be there. In the UK most of the specialists can be found at the London Early Music Exhibition, and that offers the best chance to see what is available. (Details of the exhibition, currently held annually in the autumn, are advertised in the early music magazines.) There are also regular exhibitions in Europe (Paris, Utrecht, Berlin, Regensburg and Vienna) and the USA (Boston and Berkeley in alternate years).

You should acquire catalogues of the relevant publishers. Major publishers of modern editions include Bärenreiter (publishers of the new Collected Works series of Bach, Handel and Telemann, and many editions derived from these), Breitkopf & Härtel (who published the major nineteenth-century Collected Works editions mentioned above), Schott (the London branch of the firm concentrates on recorder music), Oxford University Press (especially the *Musica da Camera* series), Wiener Urtext Edition and Henle (both concentrating on keyboard and chamber music) and the Associated Board.

Dover Books produces many volumes based on the nineteenth-century Breitkopf Collected Works. They are good value, and well produced, but of course the scholarship is not up to date. Beware of other publishers who rehash old, out-of-copyright editions, often without giving source details.

Publishers of facsimiles include J. M. Fuzeau in France, King's Music in England, Performers' Facsimiles in the USA, and Studio per Edizioni Scelte in Italy. These publish a large amount of Baroque solo and chamber music. Fuzeau issues compilations of Baroque instruction books for various instruments; the pioneering Swiss facsimile publisher Minkoff also has a wide range of early tutors. All these, as well as modern editions, can be ordered at specialist music shops or via Internet book and music shops.

The availability of editions as well as information and shopping on the Internet is likely to increase rapidly. Just because this is a new medium, do not be misled into assuming that editions that you can download necessarily fulfil the criteria suggested in this chapter. In particular, be suspicious of on-line editions that are very cheap or free, however 'clean' they may look, unless they have the authority of a reputable publisher or academic institution, and especially if no information on sources is given.

The complete editions of the major composers, and scholarly anthologies such as *Musica Britannica*, *Le Pupitre*, *Denkmäler deutscher Tonkunst*, among others, are mostly too expensive to buy, don't include any instrumental parts, and may well be too heavy to rest on a music stand. But they are useful for checking suspicious editions, and they are valuable for searching out new repertoire. They are generally only accessible in university libraries; but you will find them in some specialist public libraries – along with other help in finding out more about Baroque music and how to perform it.

Suggestions for Further Reading

The focal point of serious musical study in the English language is *The New Grove Dictionary of Music and Musicians* (London: Macmillan – good libraries should have the second edition of 2001). The article 'Performing practice' includes a section covering the period 1600 to 1750, and its bibliography gives details of many of the original sources cited by contributors to this volume. Also useful are the articles on individual instruments, which include descriptions of how the instruments developed, many illustrations, and again detailed bibliographies. In addition to its printed format, *New Grove II* is now available to subscribers on-line: if you can get access to this version through a school, college or library, you can check subject areas such as 'Performing practice' for revisions and updates.

Two useful introductory histories of the period covered by this volume are Claude V. Palisca's *Baroque Music*, 3rd edn (Englewood Cliffs, NJ: Prentice-Hall, 1991), which includes many music examples, and Nicholas Anderson's *Baroque Music: From Monteverdi to Handel* (London: Thames and Hudson, 1994), which has no music examples but many illustrations. More detailed are Manfred F. Bukofzer's *Music in the Baroque Era, from Monteverdi to Bach* (New York: W. W. Norton & Company, 1947), and two complementary volumes of The New Oxford History of Music, *V: Opera and Church Music 1630–1750* and *VI: Concert Music 1630–1750* (Oxford University Press, 1975; 1986). A more recent publication, *Companion to Baroque Music*, edited by Julie Anne Sadie (Oxford University Press, 1998), includes chapters by specialists on many topics, including performing practice.

A general study of performing is *Musical Performance: A Guide to Understanding*, edited by John Rink (Cambridge University Press, 2002). Two useful introductions to historically informed interpretation are the New Grove Handbook *Performance Practice: Music after 1600*, edited by Howard Mayer Brown and Stanley Sadie (London: Macmillan, 1989), and *The Historical Performance of Music: An Introduction*, edited by Colin Lawson and Robin Stowell (Cambridge University Press, 1999).

Large amounts of evidence concerning Baroque performance practice are assembled in two books by Robert Donington: *The Interpretation of Early Music*, 4th edn (London: Faber and Faber, 1989), and *A Performer's Guide to Baroque Music* (London: Faber and Faber, 1973). How such evidence may be applied to specific works is the subject of Peter le Huray's *Authenticity in Performance: Eighteenth-Century Case Studies* (Cambridge University Press, 1990). The evidence concerning the music of one great composer is discussed in *Bach and the Baroque: A Performing Guide to Baroque Music with Special Emphasis on the Music of J. S. Bach* by Anthony Newman (New York:

Pendragon Press, 1985). Two books concerning specific areas of performance practice (and not only of interest to wind players) are *Interpretation of French Music from 1675 to 1775, for Woodwind and other Performers* by Betty Bang Mather (New York: McGinnis & Marx, 1973), and *Free Ornamentation in Woodwind Music (1700–1775)* by Betty Bang Mather and David Lasocki (New York: McGinnis & Marx, 1976).

There is more general food for thought in Nikolaus Harnoncourt's collection of essays, talks and lectures *Baroque Music Today: Music as Speech*, translated by Mary O'Neill (Portland, Oregon: Amadeus Press; London: Christopher Helm, 1988), and in the symposium *Authenticity and Early Music*, edited by Nicholas Kenyon (Oxford University Press, 1988).

Important original sources which have appeared in modern English translations include J. J. Quantz's *On Playing the Flute*, translated by Edward R. Reilly, 2nd edn reissue (London: Faber and Faber, 2001), C. P. E. Bach's *Essay on the True Art of Playing Keyboard Instruments*, translated by William J. Mitchell (London: Eulenburg, 1974), and Leopold Mozart's *A Treatise on the Fundamental Principles of Violin Playing*, translated by Editha Knocker, 2nd edn (Oxford University Press, 1985). Despite their apparently specialist titles, all three of these contain much useful advice for all performers.

The Historical Performance of Music: An Introduction, mentioned above, is the introductory volume in a series of more specialist Cambridge Handbooks, all subtitled 'A Practical Guide'. Volumes which have appeared so far are *Early Keyboard Instruments* by David Rowland (2001), *The Early Violin and Viola* by Robin Stowell (2001), *The Early Clarinet* by Colin Lawson (2000), and *The Early Horn* by John Humphries (2000).

Cambridge University Press has also published a series of companions to different instruments (including the voice), more general in scope but still written largely from a historical perspective. The series includes: *The Cambridge Companion to the Organ*, edited by Nicholas Thistlethwaite and Geoffrey Webber (1999); *The Cambridge Companion to the Violin* and *The Cambridge Companion to the Cello*, both edited by Robin Stowell (1992; 1999); *The Cambridge Companion to the Recorder*, edited by John Mansfield Thomson and Anthony Rowland-Jones (1995); *The Cambridge Companion to the Clarinet*, edited by Colin Lawson (1995); *The Cambridge Companion to Brass Instruments*, edited by Trevor Herbert and John Wallace (1997); and *The Cambridge Companion to Singing*, edited by our contributor John Potter (2000).

The standard book on the domestic keyboard instruments of the Baroque period is Raymond Russell's *The Harpsichord and Clavichord*, 2nd edn (London: Faber and Faber, 1973). A helpful introduction is Ann Bond's *A Guide to the Harpsichord* (Portland, Oregon: Amadeus Press, 1997). For organists, the standard history, although it is now rather out of date, is William Leslie Sumner's *The Organ: Its Evolution, Principles of Construction and Use*, 4th edn (London: Macdonald and Jane's, 1973). An important French treatise of 1702 has been translated by Rebecca Harris-Warrick as *Principles of the Harpsichord by Monsieur de Saint Lambert* (Cambridge University Press, 1984). On the subject of playing continuo accompaniments see Peter Williams's *Figured Bass Accompaniment* (Edinburgh University Press, 1970).

There is a good deal about the Baroque violin in David D. Boyden's *The History of Violin Playing from its Origins to 1761* (Oxford: Clarendon Press, 1990). More general volumes are *The Amadeus Book of the Violin* by Walter Kolneder, translated by Reinhard G. Pauly (Portland, Oregon: Amadeus Press, 1998), and *The Violin Book*, edited by Richard Dawes (London: Balafon/Outline Press, 1999). Other string instruments are covered in Maurice W. Riley's two-volume *The History of the Viola* (Ann Arbor: Braun-Brumfield, Vol. 1, 2nd edn, 1993; Vol. 2, 1991), Valerie Walden's *One Hundred Years of Violoncello: A History of Technique and Performance Practice 1740–1840* (Cambridge University Press, 1998), and Harvey Turnbull's *The Guitar from the Renaissance to the Present Day* (London: Batsford, 1974).

There are two complementary general histories of wind instruments by Anthony Baines: *Woodwind Instruments and their History* (New York: Dover, 1991), and *Brass Instruments: Their History and Development* (New York: Dover, 1993). For players who do not (yet) have their own Cambridge Companions, recommended books are Nancy Toff's *The Flute Book: A Complete Guide for Students and Performers*, 2nd edn (Oxford University Press, 1997), and Günther Joppig's *The Oboe and Bassoon*, translated by Alfred Clayton (London: Batsford, 1988). Recorder players (and others) will learn a great deal from *Playing Recorder Sonatas – Interpretation and Technique* by Anthony Rowland-Jones (Oxford University Press, 1992).

Singers do have their Cambridge Companion, and may also learn a good deal from treatises of the period. Two which are available in English translation are Bénigne de Bacilly's *Remarques curieuses sur l'art de bien chanter* (1668), translated by Austin B. Caswell as *A Commentary upon the Art of Proper Singing* (New York: Institute of Medieval Music, 1968), and Pier Francesco Tosi's *Opinioni de' cantori antichi e moderni* (1723), translated by John Ernest Galliard in 1742 as *Observations on the Florid Song*, and available in a modern edition by Michael Pilkington (London: Stainer & Bell, 1987).

A clear introduction to the process of music editing is John Caldwell's *Editing Early Music*, 2nd edn (Oxford: Clarendon Press, 1995). Much more detailed is James Grier's *The Critical Editing of Music: History, Method, and Practice* (Cambridge University Press, 1996). There is a good selection of facsimiles of composers' manuscripts in *Musical Autographs from Monteverdi to Hindemith*, edited by Emanuel Winternitz (Princeton University Press, 1955; New York: Dover Publications, 1965).

Not all the books listed above are still in print; libraries may have some of them, and may be able to obtain others or suggest alternatives. Don't forget, too, that there is a great deal of information to be obtained from prefaces to editions, notes in CD booklets, magazine articles, and Internet websites. But (especially in the case of the Internet) you should always exercise your own judgement about what information is reliable and useful to you – just as you no doubt have done in reading this book.

Notes on the CD

 03.56

J. S. Bach: Sinfonia in F major BWV 1046a (original version of Brandenburg Concerto No. 1), first movement

The Academy of Ancient Music, director Christopher Hogwood

From L'Oiseau-Lyre 455 700-2, a two-disc set including Bach's six Brandenburg Concertos in their original versions

The pioneers of the Baroque revival, such as Christopher Hogwood, were interested not only in playing the music on instruments of the period (or modern copies) but also in seeking out original or alternative versions of well-known pieces – as with this 1984 recording of the original versions of the concertos which Bach brought together and revised in 1721 to present to the Margrave of Brandenburg. This movement, however, is very little different from its final version in the first Brandenburg. The orchestra consists of three oboes, bassoon, two *corni da caccia* (natural horns), solo strings and harpsichord. Notice that the horns play triplet figures, probably real hunting-calls, which do not fit in with the other rhythms.

 03.39

Monteverdi: *Orfeo*, excerpt from Act II

John Mark Ainsley (tenor), New London Consort, director Philip Pickett

From L'Oiseau-Lyre 433 545-2, a two-disc set of the complete opera as it might have been heard at its first performance

Orfeo is grief-stricken at the news of the death of his new bride, but resolves to go to Hades to try to win her back with his singing; the chorus comments on the fleeting nature of human happiness. See Ex. 1.2, and George Pratt's commentary on pp. 4–6 on the expressive dissonances of this passage, the use of continuo accompaniment, and the rhetorical declamation in the vocal part. Notice also the contrast between Orfeo's new-style recitative and the choral writing, which in style and texture is closer to the Renaissance madrigal tradition.

 02.49

Rameau: *Castor et Pollux*, first section of the aria 'Tristes apprêts' from Act I

Agnes Mellon (soprano), Les Arts Florissants, conductor William Christie

From Harmonia Mundi HMC 901435-37, a three-disc set of the complete opera

Télaïra is inconsolable at the death of her beloved Castor, king of Sparta. The extract shows the distinctive qualities of French Baroque vocal music, with its sensitivity to the stresses of the French language and its delicate ornamentation. The obbligato bassoon part is typical of Rameau's imaginative ear for instrumental colour.

 03.40

Purcell: *The Fairy Queen*, beginning of The Plaint in the masque for Act V

Kym Amps (soprano), Robin Canter (oboe), The Scholars Baroque Ensemble, director David van Asch

From Naxos 8.550660 (HNH International Ltd), a two-disc set of Purcell's complete music for this 'semi-opera'

Another lament for a lost love, this time by an English composer. Its obbligato part is often played on the violin, but is now recognized as intended for the oboe. The first section is over a repeating 'ground bass'; the second section (from 02.02) is freely composed.

 03.48

Handel: *Joshua*, scene in recitative from Act I

Emma Kirkby (soprano), James Bowman (countertenor), The King's Consort, conductor Robert King

From Hyperion CDA 66461/2, a two-disc set of the complete oratorio

The young warrior Othniel walks through a beautiful landscape in search of Achsah, his betrothed, and the couple are united. Othniel is sung by a countertenor, or male alto. Notice the contrast between accompanied recitative, in regular rhythm and with orchestral accompaniment, and the more normal kind of recitative, in free time following the rhythm of the words, and with continuo accompaniment only.

01.27

Michelangelo Rossi: Toccata No. 7, final section

Sophie Yates (harpsichord)

From Chandos Chaconne CHAN 0601, Romanesca, a collection of Italian music of the seventeenth and eighteenth centuries, played on a single-manual harpsichord by Ransom and Hammet after early Italian models

See Ex. 2.1, p. 24. As Peter Holman has observed, the unequal semitones of mean-tone (or ¼-comma mean-tone) tuning give the final section of this toccata a 'strange and almost bizarre' quality. You may need to listen to this track a few times to overcome the initial impression, to ears used to equal temperament, that this passage is simply 'out of tune'.

01.20

J. S. Bach: French Overture in B minor BWV 831, start of the first movement, Ouverture

Christophe Rousset (harpsichord)

From L'Oiseau-Lyre 433 054-2, containing music by Bach, played on a harpsichord made by Henri Hemsch in Paris in 1751

Bach's 'French Overture' is a keyboard imitation of French-style orchestral dance suites of the time. From the notation of the opening section, it is clear that Bach intended it to be played in the jerky, 'over-dotted' French-overture manner described by Peter Holman on pp. 41–2.

00.59

J. S. Bach: Suite No. 1 in C major BWV 1066, start of the Ouverture

The Brandenburg Consort, director Roy Goodman

From Hyperion CDD 22002, a two-disc set including all four of Bach's 'orchestral' suites, in fact played by an ensemble of soloists

Although the opening movement of this French-style dance suite is called 'Ouverture', its combination of dotted quavers with regular semiquaver movement makes general 'over-dotting' impossible. However, in this performance dotted crotchets are still played double-dotted; and notice that the players adopt a brisk tempo and insert rests in the dotted figures, to give the same overall effect of liveliness and crispness.

02.46

Corelli: Sonata in B flat major Op. 5 No. 2, first movement, Grave

Elizabeth Wallfisch (violin), Richard Tunnicliffe (cello), Paul Nicholson (organ)

From Hyperion CDA 66381/2, a two-disc set of Corelli's complete Op. 5 sonatas

See Ex. 2.22, p. 47. This performance is freely based on the edition of the Op. 5 sonatas published in Amsterdam in 1710, with ornamented versions of the slow movements which the publisher claimed were 'composed by Corelli as he plays them'. Whether or not these 'graces' are indeed Corelli's own, they are typical of the florid ornamentation applied to slow movements at the time.

04.13

J. S. Bach: *Das wohltemperirte Clavier* Book 1, Prelude and Fugue in B major

Colin Tilney (clavichord)

From a four-disc Hyperion set (currently unavailable) of the complete *Das wohltemperirte Clavier* played on clavichord and harpsichord; the clavichord was made by J. A. Hass of Hamburg in 1767

The clavichord gives the different lines of the prelude a singing quality, and clarifies the four-part texture of the fugue. If you can, try listening to this track on headphones with the volume turned low – the clavichord is a very quiet and private instrument.

04.19

J. S. Bach: *Das wohltemperirte Clavier* Book 2, Prelude and Fugue in C major

Davitt Moroney (harpsichord)

From Harmonia Mundi Musique d'Abord HMA 1901285-88, a four-disc set of the complete *Das wohltemperirte Clavier*, played on a modern harpsichord, by John Phillips, in the Baroque tradition

The harpsichord has a more extrovert quality than the clavichord, well suited to the prelude and fugue that begins Book 2.

04.15

J. S. Bach: *Das wohltemperirte Clavier* Book 2, Prelude and Fugue in E flat major

Angela Hewitt (piano)

From Hyperion CDA 67303/4, a two-disc set of the second book of the 'forty-eight'

Angela Hewitt is one of the most admired present-day interpreters of Bach on the modern piano. She plays this gentle prelude and sterner fugue with clear textures and phrasing, but without any attempt to imitate the sound of earlier instruments.

02.46

Louis Couperin: *Prélude à l'imitation de Monsieur Froberger* (in A minor), first section

Davitt Moroney (harpsichord)

From a four-disc Harmonia Mundi set (not currently available in the UK) of the complete harpsichord music of Louis Couperin, played on several different instruments

This is one possible realization of the 'unmeasured prelude' shown in Ex. 3.2, p. 53, in which the length and duration of the notes are left to the player. The instrument is a two-manual harpsichord made by Albert Delin in Tournai in 1768, tuned at very low pitch (a' = 392) in an unequal temperament.

02.17

Froberger: Toccata in D minor, first section

Davitt Moroney (organ)

From a Harmonia Mundi disc (not currently available in the UK) of organ music by Froberger, played on the Dallam organ in Lanvellac

This toccata is preserved in the well-known Bauyn manuscript, which is one of the main sources of keyboard music by French composers, as well as some visitors to France such as the German Froberger. In that manuscript it is described as 'composed in Brussels, 1650'. The piece is a good example of the 'free' or 'fantastic' style of seventeenth-century music, although it is hardly as free as the piece 'in imitation of Froberger' which precedes it here. The organ in this recording is the oldest working instrument (in its original state) in France. It was built by the English organ-builder Robert Dallam while he was working in Britanny in 1653, and is now in the parish church of Lanvellac.

02.29

Lully, arr. d'Anglebert: *Chaconne de Galatée*

Davitt Moroney (harpsichord)

From Hyperion CDA 67164, containing Marc Roger Normand Couperin's complete *Livre de Tablature de Clavecin*, played on a copy by John Phillips of a 1697 harpsichord by Nicolas Dumont

This piece in chaconne time was originally a dance in Lully's opera *Acis et Galatée*. Like many popular operatic numbers, it was soon arranged for harpsichord, in this case by Jean Henry d'Anglebert. This version, which differs in key and other respects from d'Anglebert's published arrangement of 1689, is from a manuscript collection assembled by Marc Roger Normand Couperin, a nephew of Louis Couperin and cousin of François 'le grand'. In this performance, notice the delicacy of the ornamentation, and the flexibility of the rhythm: quavers are sometimes equal, sometimes dotted, and often somewhere in between (*notes inégales*).

02.46

Buxtehude: In dulci jubilo, BuxWV 197

Piet Kee (organ)

From Chandos Chaconne CHAN 0514, consisting of organ music by Buxtehude and Sweelinck, played on the organ of St Laurens, Alkmaar

Buxtehude was organist of St Mary's, Lübeck for nearly forty years until his death in 1707. This chorale prelude by him is based on the Christmas hymn 'In dulci jubilo', richly ornamented. The organ, in the parish church of Alkmaar in the Netherlands, dates originally from 1639–46, but was rebuilt by the famous north German organ-builder Franz Caspar Schnitger between 1723 and 1725; recently restored, it is one of the finest examples of the northern European Baroque organ.

02.09

Giovanni Paolo Cima: *Sonata per il violino*, first section

Romanesca: Andrew Manze (violin), Nigel North (theorbo), John Toll (chamber organ)

From Harmonia Mundi HMU 907211, Phantasticus, a collection of seventeenth-century Italian violin music

See Ex. 4.1, p. 70, and Andrew Manze's comments on the first publication of sonatas specifically for the violin. Notice the freedom of tempo associated with the 'stylus phantasticus', and also the effective continuo section of theorbo and chamber organ.

03.24

J. S. Bach: Concerto in D minor for two violins BWV 1043, first movement

Andrew Manze (violin/director), Rachel Podger (violin), The Academy of Ancient Music

From Harmonia Mundi HMU 907155, a disc of Bach concertos for one and two violins

See Ex. 4.6, p. 77. In this well-known movement, notice the lightness and flexibility of articulation which can be achieved with Baroque instruments and Baroque bows.

02.27

Vivaldi: Sonata in B flat major RV 46, first movement, Preludio: Largo

David Watkins (cello), members of The King's Consort

From Hyperion CDA 66881/2, a two-disc set of Vivaldi's complete sonatas for cello and continuo

The cello was used more often for continuo accompaniment than as a solo instrument during the Baroque period; but there are many concertos and sonatas for it by the prolific Antonio Vivaldi. In this recording notice the expressive quality achieved by the solo cellist with minimal use of vibrato, and his subtle decoration of the return of the opening melody. Notice also the continuo section of a second cello on the bass line, theorbo and chamber organ.

20 02.16

Handel: *Music for the Royal Fireworks*, fourth movement, 'La Réjouissance'

The King's Consort, conductor Robert King

From Hyperion CDA 66350, containing the *Music for the Royal Fireworks* and Handel's four coronation anthems

This festive movement is played by a period-instrument band corresponding to the enormous ensemble which is known to have been assembled for the first, outdoor performance: nine trumpets, nine horns, twenty-four oboes, twelve bassoons and kettledrums.

21 03.11

Telemann: Concerto in E minor for recorder and flute, third movement, Largo

John Turner (recorder), Stephen Preston (flute), The Academy of Ancient Music, director Christopher Hogwood

From L'Oiseau-Lyre 411 949-2, a collection of concertos by Telemann

This slow movement allows a chance to compare the recorder with the 'German' or transverse flute which gradually supplanted it during the eighteenth century. Notice that the two instruments are more alike in tone-colour and, especially, volume than their modern counterparts. Notice also the gentle pizzicato accompaniment.

22 02.25

Matthew Locke: For His Majestys Sagbutts and Cornetts, Pavan-Almand a 6

His Majestys Sagbutts and Cornetts

From Hyperion CDA 66894, also called For His Majestys Sagbutts and Cornetts, a collection of English music from Henry VIII to Charles II

A familiar Renaissance and early Baroque ensemble consisted of cornetts, curved instruments with brass mouthpieces and woodwind fingering, and sackbuts, early trombones. Some of the last music written for these instruments was composed by Matthew Locke at the court of King Charles II; his collection includes this solemn dance for two cornetts and four sackbuts. Players of modern brass instruments tackling this repertoire should aim for some of the same smoothness of articulation and phrasing.

23 02.48

Handel: *Messiah*, first section of the aria 'He was despised'

Anne Sofie von Otter (mezzo-soprano), The English Concert, conductor Trevor Pinnock

From Archiv 423 630-2, a two-disc set of the complete oratorio

This aria is at the centre of John Potter's chapter on singing, and is reproduced as Exx. 6.1–3, pp. 96–9. Anne Sofie von Otter, one of the most celebrated and versatile singers of the present day, is unlikely to sound at all like the first performer of the aria, the actress Mrs Cibber; but her performance is certainly capable of moving us, as Mrs Cibber's did her contemporaries.

24 02.52

Gottfried Heinrich Stölzel: Bist du bei mir

John Potter (tenor), Tragicomedia: Erin Headley (viola da gamba), Stephen Stubbs (lute)

From Teldec Das Alte Werk 4509 91183 2 containing a selection from Bach's *Das Notenbüchlein für Anna Magdalena Bach*

By permission of Warner Classics, Warner Music UK and Warner Strategic Marketing. From Das Alte Werk ℗ 1994 Teldec Classics International GmbH. www.warnerclassics.com

The song, for many years attributed to Bach, begins: 'When you are with me, I go in joy to death and peace'. John Potter sings it in an intimate manner appropriate to music-making within the Bach family circle, accompanied by viola da gamba and lute.

25 02.13

Pietro Antonio Locatelli: Sonata in G minor Op. 2 No. 6, fourth movement, Allegro

Il Ruggiero

From Tactus TC 691202, containing the first six of Locatelli's Op. 2 sonatas

See Exx. 7.1–2, pp. 109–10, and Clifford Bartlett's discussion of a modern edition of this movement and the very different original version. The performers on this recording – on flute, cello and harpsichord – were playing from facsimile reprints of the 1732 publication.